# LIVING

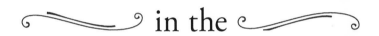 in the

# LAND OF I AM

YOUR LIFE STORY REVEALS YOUR PURPOSE

## TIFFANY JAMES

Living in the Land of I Am
Your Life Story Reveals Your Purpose

Copyright © 2019 by Tiffany James

ISBN   978-0-578-46129-8 (paperback)
       978-0-578-50665-4 (hardcover)

Published by Encouraging Touch Enterprise

Edited by Christy Distler, Avodah Editorial Services
Front cover photo by Jesse James
Cover and interior design by Jera Publishing

## White Canvas

WHAT IF I CLOSED my eyes and saw the sky as a white canvas waiting for the imagination of my soul to freely paint the unseen beauty of creation?

I would paint the strength of the sun, the humility of the moon, and the authority of the air. I would paint the harmony of the hummingbird, the voice of its wings as they brush against the wind. I would paint the laughter of a little child's first tickle, the excitement of their first Christmas, and the blush of their first kiss. I would paint a smooth jazz melody during a midnight summer breeze, I would paint the fragrance of an everlasting love, and I would paint the gentleness of a peacock's feather. I would paint the conversations of the clouds, I would paint the joy of the morning, the newness of a day and the possibilities of tomorrow. I would paint the cure for cancer and the secret to youth. I would paint the end to war, while painting the awareness of peace. I would paint the determination of the spirit, the wisdom of Solomon, and the poise of confidence. I would paint the breath of the Creator; His unseen hand in creation. I would paint the beauty of the beholder, the softness of His touch, the radiance of His being, and the sovereignty of His love. I would paint the unseen truth of real beauty, the twinkle of an eye, and the mystery of greatness.

I would paint the foundation of faith, how to dream big with God and walk with the imagination of the soul wide open "for nothing will be impossible with God."

TIFFANY JAMES

# CONTENTS

# ACKNOWLEDGEMENTS

To my Unseen Hero: You never stop believing in me. You encouraged, tested, loved, and sowed into me. You have been my Best Friend, the Lover of my soul, my Everything. Thank you for life.

To myself: You did it, you believed, you were bold and courageous, and you jumped! I love the woman you have become.

To my girls: May this book be one of the greatest gifts I could give you. It's my voice that I pray you forever carry with you. I want you to love yourselves, believe in yourselves, and be who you were created to be unapologetically. Never compare yourselves to anyone, because each of you is a beautiful rare specimen on earth. You all will forever be my angels and I am so proud to be your mom.

To my amazing husband: Thank you for always allowing me to be myself, no questions asked. You have provided for me while I held on to dear life for my dreams. I am proud to be your wife and you will forever hold the key to my heart.

To my dreamers: I want to be the courage that causes your dreams to become a reality. Yes, dreams really do come true. So, believe in them because they will always believe in you and so will I.

To Bernie: There are no words. Thank you for being trustworthy and truthful throughout this book project. Your wisdom is immeasurable.

To my brother-in-love, Jesse, thank you for capturing such a powerful picture of me. You are such a gifted photographer. I love and appreciate you.

To my mom and dad: I am truly grateful that God blessed me with you both. I would not be who I am today without you. I hope I make you proud. Love you madly.

To all my mentors, spiritual moms, my spiritual dad, close friends, my two best friends and family: Thank each of you for praying for me and believing with me. You know how much I love you because I've made it a point to always let you know. Whatever dreams you have that you have not boldly stepped into, you can't wait any longer. I laid the stones of faith so that you can boldly walk in your purpose.

To every organization, every church, and everyone who believed in me and gave me an opportunity to use my voice to encourage others—Thank you! You are all a part of my journey!

# FOREWORD

Tiffany James, known to me as "My Li'l Encourager," is no stranger to the written word. She has the ability to say the things we all wish we could express. With encouragement for every situation, her relatable and inspiring words can bridge the gap from one generation to another.

In *Living in the Land of I Am*, a breathtaking work of storytelling, Tiffany draws on a diverse array of real-life experiences. She weaves together the stories of her life, creating a complex tapestry of politics, love, and friendship amidst a crumbling society. Her emotional richness, honesty, and transparency will engage you.

Because of her faith and God-given gifts of encouragement, wisdom, and knowledge, she can peer into the heart of mankind and see where we have fallen short in what God has desired and designed for us. It is this task of discovering who we are and the path that we must travel in order to know God, find freedom, discover our purpose, and make a difference, that has prompted her to pen *Living in the Land of I Am*.

As you journey to *Living in the Land of I Am*, you will encounter profound insights on every page, stories that will make you examine the way you work, the way you lead, and the impact you have on the world. Tiffany unpacks stories of failure that illustrate what not to do, as well as identifies common pitfalls we all encounter, and then she shares how easy it is to fall prey to a toxic culture that seeks to define who we are and insists we live life in an age of constant pressure to conform and pretend.

Tiffany has discovered that many of us have allowed our experiences, challenges, failures, gifts, talents and abilities, and even people and struggles to define and dictate our very existence. Life, as many have come to conclude, is the ability to "just survive." But she declares, "I believed and served hell notice that survival would be my starting line, not my finish line."

As we travel with the writer, Tiffany reveals that our perception of who we are is crucial to living out our purpose: "Perception is a devourer of truth. It blinds us to a greater reality. We're moved by what we see and hear, never taking the time to really understand and look beyond our emotions. Perspective is everything."

As she invites you to follow her journey in life, you will gain valuable insights that will help you travel to a place where you can be who you were truly designed to be. You can discover the benefits that are afforded and the power one possesses when living a life of purpose. No matter your age or your current status in life, this book will make you ponder the question,

Am I living in the Land of I am? I encourage you to take the journey to discovering your purpose and living your best life in the Land of I am.

I have no doubt you will be blessed.

DR. BARBARA J. WILLIAMS
Coauthor, *Change Your Life,*
*90 Day Experience – The Path to Your Destiny*

# INTRODUCTION

*Living in the Land of I Am* is powerful truth about being and embracing your true authentic self. It's my story and it's your story.

Have you ever watched the movie *The Ten Commandments*? It's an all-time classic about a Hebrew man by the name of Moses, who as an infant was put in a basket and placed in the Nile River by his mother and sister to escape a decree by Pharaoh to kill all Hebrew male babies. The backstory is that Pharaoh was threatened by a prophecy that a deliverer from the Hebrew people would come to overthrow him and free the Hebrews, who had been enslaved under Egypt's rule for over five hundred years. Ironically, Moses was rescued by Pharaoh's daughter (unbeknownst to Pharaoh) and raised as a great, beloved Egyptian prince.

As an adult, Moses learns the truth: He was not born an Egyptian prince, the mother he adores and loves is not his real mother, and his whole life has been a lie. At a critical and devastating moment in his life, he has a choice to make. He can keep this a secret, or he can embrace who he really is and research his biological roots.

Moses chooses to embrace his true identity, and life as he knows it is never the same. The movie is a must-see and it's quite long, so of course I can't fully summarize it, but in short Moses does discover his biological and cultural roots. He is also disowned and banned from Egypt and sent out into the wilderness to die. Egypt attempts to erase Moses from their royal history.

Even so, Moses survives the tortures of the wilderness and ultimately learns more about himself than his ethnicity; he discovers his purpose. Everything that happened from the palace of Egypt to the desert of the Midian plains has all been for a divine purpose.

During one of the most memorable parts of the movie, Moses, who is now married, a father, and living his life as a shepherd, sees on top of a mountain a fire burning but not consuming anything and is compelled to go see it. When he reaches the mountaintop, he takes off his shoes, realizing he stands on holy ground before God. The Lord speaks to him, explaining that Moses is the chosen one who will deliver the Hebrew slaves from the hands of the Egyptians. At first, Moses questions God's choice because he doesn't feel qualified for such a purpose. God reassures Moses that He will be with him.

Moses then asks, "When I go, who shall I say sent me?" God's response is powerful and unlimited: "I AM WHO I AM." He goes on to say, "Tell them, 'I AM sent me.'"

Years later, God's response to Moses of who He was would become the foundation of my identity. God was making a profound statement to Moses to not marginalize or minimize Him to a title or name. I felt like He was saying, "I am everything I want and need to be at any given time." Likewise, God was saying to me, "You can be and do whatever I've purposed for your life." This is what "Living in the Land of I Am" means: Living and being your true authentic self ... learning through different season and situations who you were created to be. It's loving and nurturing yourself. The land is you!

Have you ever been asked, "Who do you think you are?" when you decide to take a risk and do something outside the norm? Have you ever talked yourself out of doing something because those words echoed in your mind? We spend most of our lives trying to answer the big question of "Who am I?" Like Moses, regardless of our backstory, we must find the courage to step into the truth of who we were created to be. Moses moved out, not in his own ability and strength, but in the truth of I am!

I am is a truth that forever changed my life.

On January 19, 2016, while sitting on my couch, I realized I was not living. Have you ever had a moment when you literally couldn't breathe—choking on the fumes of disappointment, trying to find the exit door so you can escape the flames of failure you're feeling? On this day, I came to see that I had lived for everyone else, doing anything and everything to feel complete and accepted. Surely there had to be more to life than this?

I knew the answer was yes, but fear made it impossible for me to find the exit door of faith. My friends, I was suffocating, suffocating, suffocating, I declare! Trying to catch my breath. Trying to figure out where did forty-something years of my life go? I'm surprised I'm still alive.

How could I have been afraid of my own greatness—afraid of being myself? All these years, I'd felt like I lacked that "something special," the "it factor" that makes a person great. I knew I had gifts, but I also convinced myself that what I possessed wasn't good enough. So I hid for most of my life, crouching behind a lie that became my crutch. Being not good enough gave me an excuse to not go after the "more" even if there was more.

I never really embraced or even recognized that being my true authentic self was the definition of greatness. Finally, I'd reached a place where I was no longer comfortable hiding, no longer satisfied with being what I thought other people expected me to be. I think I always knew there was more but admitting that truth would cause me to come out of hiding and get rid of my excuses. I would have to be bold enough to step out in front of millions of people, strike a Wonder Woman pose, and say, "Go, Tiffany! Go, Tiffany! Go!"

According to actor and comedian Steve Harvey, "If you are waking up with the sensation that there has got to be more in life ... then there is."[1] When you begin to accept and embrace who you were created to be, fear ceases to have a passport in your world. The giants of intimidation are annihilated. Living in the Land of I am is where you and you alone reign by finding out who you were created to be and then, with full authority, owning it.

When I think about the Land of I am, I liken it to an inherited parcel of land. You have the freedom to build and grow whatever you desire because you now own the land. It's where you take the time to get rid of anything that will invade, destroy, or try to rule your land. It's where you begin to learn the history of the land, because when you don't know your history, you're doomed to repeat it. This means learning why you made the choices you made (good and bad), because your choices and the consequences that follow can become a much-needed map on your journey to becoming your best self.

When you find yourself struggling with your identity, you can study the map of your land. You must re-examine your soil (foundation), because a lot of what we believe comes from it. Did you know that soil is alive? It's your beginning, and much of your growth comes from this beginning. Have there been times when you tried to rebuild or fix a structure and it didn't work? Well, it's probably because you had a faulty foundation. Without a strong, solid foundation, sooner or later what you've built will eventually collapse under the weight of life.

I want you to realize that there is more to you than meets the eye. So, stop existing and start living. You were strategically designed for a purpose. When you realize your purpose, you're better able to understand who you are. Your identity and your purpose were woven into a beautiful tapestry by God before you were born. Understanding the needlework of God, trying to trace the threads of His design for your life, can be an exciting yet complex expedition. You might not ever fully comprehend the brilliance of His design, but you can learn how to discover the hidden beauty within it. Self-discovery is just that—a beautiful journey of learning oneself. You are who God says you are.

I hope to encourage you through my own journey of how I discovered and embraced my true authentic self. To do that, I'll share with you where I used to be, where I am now, and, most of all, where God desires you to be.

"When you can't find the
courage to jump allow
yourself to be pushed."

—*Tiffany James*

# CHAPTER ONE

# How it all Happened

Did I jump or was I pushed? If you're reading this book, it means I jumped. It means I was tired of sitting in the plane, parachute and all my expensive fly gear on, the door of the plane open, staring out with the fresh wind hitting my face (saying to myself, *This is what the air tastes like one thousand feet up in air*). The real question should have been, *Am I crazy? Out-of-my-mind crazy?*

I was laughing because I'd lost count of how many times I got to this point but never jumped. Heart pounding, no turning back, I tried to convince myself to jump even though I knew I'd been here before. Flashes of death, every stupid question coming to my mind. *Will an eagle swallow me whole if I jump out of this plane? Will my body disintegrate before I hit the ground if my parachute doesn't open? Will people laugh at me if I die? How many would say they knew it would end this way?*

Thoughts can be a dream killer.

I was squatting at the open plane door, looking out into the beautiful sky of freedom. I was prepared, excited, scared, determined ... and did I say scared? Yet I was still sitting until three days later. I'm not sure if I jumped or if Steve Harvey pushed me.

You're probably laughing, but I'm serious. That crazy, fun, genuine comedian, actor, author, game show host, radio broadcaster, TV show host, producer (did you know Steve Harvey even had his own record label once?), motivational speaker, mentor, and I'm sure I left something out ... but that crazy man in one of his rare moments of seriousness had the nerve to push me!

Or did I jump? Either way, I was out of the plane, air hitting my face hard, but it was exhilarating, life changing, and liberating. This is one decision I will never regret. I know you're saying, "Don't leave us hanging! How did you get Steve Harvey to push you—or as you say, jump?"

I hear your sarcasm and I must say I like it. Let me explain: Three days after my couch moment, I received a text from a friend, on Friday, January 22, 2016 with a link and this message: "Tiffany, did you see this?? This video is evvvverrthing!!" It was a video of Steve Harvey talking to a live audience before the TV show *Family Feud* started, an unaired clip explaining that to become successful in life, to go from existing to living, you must jump. How did Steve know I was in the airplane, scared to death to jump? I'm not sure what happened, honestly, but I can tell you that by the end of the video, I was out of that plane.

Now I know you're saying, "Tell us what happened! Don't leave us hanging, for goodness' sake. How often is it that someone gets pushed out of a plane, and by Steve Harvey of all people?"

This book you're holding in your hand is what happened next. In it you'll learn a lot about me, but one thing I want to tell you up-front is that I use dramatized storytelling and inspirational spoken word to encourage you through the chapters of this book. I've always loved a little drama—it makes every story a bit better—and I love to use my life experiences to not only encourage, inspire, and empower, but to also give wisdom.

One of my inspirational stories is called "I Did Not Know My Own Strength." I originally wrote this piece in 2010 for a book release gala for a non-profit organization called Women on Pursuit. This organization was founded by my friend Kim Weaver to support and empower women from all walks of life. The book was a collaboration of different women's stories of remaining whole despite adversity. My friend's vision was that I would read the book and write a storytelling piece and present it at the conference before the guest speaker, author Terry McMillan, came forth, which was such a huge honor. As I read, I found a common thread. I put the book down and began to write:

## I Didn't Know
## My Own Strength

I'VE WAITED ON THIS day for such a long time. I've played it again and again in the forefront of my mind: the day I finally get to tell my story like so many of those who have gone before me. I guess I need to start from the very beginning, because for as long as I can remember, I have always thought myself to be a phenomenal woman and understood that the world hadn't noticed me yet (said with my Maya Angelou attitude and my fierce two-step, and ending with that model stand-still pose). I always knew I was gifted with unlimited possibilities, I just hadn't been discovered by the right opportunities. I was one who once dreamed even though many tried to keep me awake.

Yes, you're looking at a woman who once truly believed in herself (more attitude), but somewhere along the way I got stagnated by the voices playing in my head, reminding me again and again what the last person said—that I was weak, useless, and insecure. Some even called me ugly, said I would never find anyone who truly loved me, and said that no matter what I tried to accomplish in life, I would never amount to nothing. And after so long, those voices somehow became my truth and all those things I once thought myself to be were no longer clear to me. See, this is my story, but it's not unique. My story has been sung in countless songs, acted out on the big screen, and told in books and magazines. Even so, not enough people have woken up to the struggles that so many of us face today.

———————•  •———————

I'll stop right there; it's a long piece. When I performed this reading a second time, at a different event, I realized something: the women's stories were mine. Our common thread was that we didn't know who we were anymore, and some of us never knew in the first place.

Like so many others, I spent over half of my life trying to figure out who the hell I was and years after struggling to accept my new findings. I realized that we can never reach our true destiny without first knowing our true identity. I'm not sure when, where, or even how I lost contact with who I was created to be, but I did. However, Steve Harvey, through the video my friend texted me, gave me the courage to share my journey of self-discovery, as well as self-acceptance.

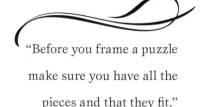

"Before you frame a puzzle
make sure you have all the
pieces and that they fit."

*—Tiffany James*

CHAPTER TWO

# Perspective Is Everything

I have an amazing memory. So why is it that I can't remember a lot of my childhood? Why can't I remember what's supposed to be the most precious and fun years of life? Recently, my dad was sharing some childhood memories with me and pointing out how spoiled I was. As beautiful as the stories were, I didn't remember any of them. Crazy!

I have to wonder if I can't remember because at some time during my childhood I was taken from the Land of I am and placed in the Land of Whoever You Need or Want Me to Be. I look at childhood photos with no memory of that time or experience in my life. I used to be afraid to admit this because it would force me to think about what could have happened to me that I can't remember. Did something tragic happen? Was I protecting myself from the experience? Or was I a loved and cherished child but my difficult teenage years erased that reality? I often wonder if my parents saw amazing things about me as a child, some special gift or ability. Was there a certain peculiar pizazz about me? Was I a friendly, talkative child? Well, I *know* I was a talkative child, that I remember. But was I so peculiar that I was misunderstood and rejected?

I went back to school part time in 2015, taking a speech class with an emphasis on storytelling. We were given our first assignment, which was to tell a personal story from our childhood, complete with an outline to help us formulate the sequence of events as they transpired. The story was to be about an upside-down event—an occurrence that changed our "normal" in some way and the impact created a "new normal," altering our behavior/thinking. I wondered, *Could I have had an upside-down event that I don't remember that forever changed the way I thought about myself?*

One memory that stood out took place when I was in fifth grade. A friend passed out at school due to the heat that day, and I was really concerned and started to cry. I kneeled beside her and held her hand, not realizing the laughing eyes all around me. When I returned to my classroom, whispers, rude jokes, and hurtful remarks from my peers awaited.

This confused me. I couldn't understand why no one embraced the beauty of my personality—why no one saw being compassionate and caring as a good thing. As a matter of fact, it was quite the opposite; they all despised me instead. Everything I had been to them was gone in an instant, and my friends abandoned me for being me.

It's easy for people to say, "Don't worry about what others say. You know who you are." But when you're a child and you just want to be liked and loved, only to be treated with contempt by those you call family and friends, the scars can be so small and yet so deep.

Even though no one saw it, I was carrying a deep seed of rejection and it stayed with me. I hated being someone who people thought of as "weird," so I decided that day that being me was not enough or acceptable to the world. This was now my new norm, and I began to become the very thing I despised. I acted outside my character, becoming rude, disrespectful, wild, and mean. Every day I was losing touch with the real me—and losing touch with the unique gift that God planted in me from my mother's womb: to be *different*.

Have you ever lost something so small but so valuable in a pile of dirt or maybe on the playground when you were growing up? It's like trying to find a needle in a haystack. The one word that comes to mind is *frustrated*. You get the same feeling when you lose yourself in this messed-up world. You find yourself frustrated with being you, and ask yourself, *"Where do I begin to look?"* When you don't know your own identity, someone else can easily come into your life and define you. That's where I lost myself. I looked for validation from everyone else.

I believe I was always different but never truly realized it until fifth grade. After this event, I questioned everything about myself. I started to see that everyone thought I was different in a negative way. At home, there were things said about me that I perceived as negative; my family not knowing that these things were only adding to the labels that had been put on me at school. I also felt like I was always compared to my older sister and that I came up short in my mom's eyes.

It made me feel like my sister possessed something awesome that deserved to be nurtured, while I was different but in an undesirable way. Eventually, the stance I took at school became the same one I took at home. I was tired of trying to measure up and falling short time and time again.

Now let's take a moment to define *different*, because many people today look at being different as a negative thing. The *Encarta World English Dictionary* defines *different* as "unlike something or somebody else, distinct: separate or distinct from another or others, unusual: contrary to norms or expectations."[2]

As a child, I didn't know the definition of *different*, so other people defined it for me. It could mean strange, weird, unacceptable, disliked, odd, unattractive, loud, confused, nerdy, fast, black, or a host of other things. I was always considered different in the negative sense of the word and called all the above and so much more.

I was very talkative, but instead of people seeing that as a positive quality (by, for example, encouraging me to become a motivational speaker or maybe even a lawyer), I was told, "You need to shut up. You talk too much, and people don't care for loud-mouthed talkative girls." They didn't realize that talking came naturally to me and that it brought me joy to speak, no matter who I was talking to or where I was. I was never nervous or afraid. For that reason, being quiet felt foreign to me. So, it's not a coincidence that today I use my voice to encourage people into their destiny.

I also loved to play softball, football, and volleyball, and I loved to run, but because these sports involved boys, I was labeled what grown-ups would call a girl who was trying to grow up to soon, "fast." I often heard, "No one wants to be around a fast-ass little girl." The funny thing is that at the time, sex was the furthest thing from my mind, and no boy had even approached me yet.

I had dark skin and coarse, thick, long black hair, and was often called *blackie, raisin bran, chocolate,* and *rat.* These were my nicknames given to me by my family, and while I'm sure they didn't mean any harm, what was a young girl to think? What a difference the words *beautiful, precious,* or *sweet* would have made for me.

I had this thing for being righteous and I was always direct, but that was looked upon as talking back and having a bad attitude. But what if that character trait meant I was blessed with wisdom beyond my years? It could have meant that I was sensitive and alert to the things that weren't fair or just.

I often wonder, if my personality had been embraced and nurtured in a positive way growing up, what effect it would have had on my self-esteem and growth. What if my parents had taken the time to study me so they could help me better understand who I was created to be?

I'm now a parent, and I realize how easy it is for any parent to want to correct what we feel isn't appropriate in our children. But in our duties of trying to make sure our children are behaving properly and accepted by society, we often fail to recognize and embrace their uniqueness. We fail to love our children for who they are. God makes no mistakes, and He didn't create any of us to waste us. We already must face a world that tries to define us, and often children must face that world at a huge disadvantage.

In Jerry Minchinton's book *Maximum Self-Esteem*, he states that when we entered the world as babies, it was with a clean slate, so to speak. We knew absolutely nothing about ourselves, good or bad. Since in our unselfconscious state, we had no reason to dislike ourselves, we automatically had high self-esteem. He goes on to write that this blissful state of ignorance was only temporary. Like tiny sponges, our minds soon began to soak up information about ourselves from our parents and our environment. With the input we received, we began fashioning the self-image that would follow us into our adult life.

This was my case, and it may be yours. I don't have a sad story, because in hindsight I know my parents raised me to the best of their ability. You can't give out what you don't have. I remember telling my mom that I wanted kids (girls) and that I would never yell at my kids the way she yelled at me. Well, shamefully, I must confess that with my eldest, I found myself dealing with her in the same way my mom dealt with me. I never knew any other way, and how can one learn unless one has a teacher? My mom didn't have a mother figure to teach her how to deal with a child/teenager/young adult, especially one like me. Remember, I was unique—a rare specimen. (I'm laughing at myself.)

I was a child and didn't have the ability to recognize what was or wasn't sown into my parents when they were growing up. Then as I got older and more mature, I learned a lot about my parents' upbringing. Looking back now with newfound information, I have a totally different perspective. I can honestly say my parents were wounded soldiers and my unsung heroes. They still tried to fight without any weapons, and they tried to fly as parents even though they didn't have the cape or superpowers to do so.

In my storytelling class, I had another speech project that entailed choosing someone I admire and telling their story as a first-person narrative. I chose a woman who I truly love and admire, Maya Angelou, however, I ended up telling her mother's story instead. I had learned that Vivian Baxter was the force behind Maya Angelou's voice, and that if Maya had never told her story, we wouldn't know who took Maya from being a mute, scared little girl to the strong, phenomenal woman she became. Maya celebrated her mom, but the world never saw her. Yet hidden in the history of Maya's life, there you will find Vivian.

I've come to realize that parents are often the most misunderstood and underappreciated people in the world. They are the ones who still show up even when they're forgotten. They carry the ability to love unconditionally, even if their actions don't always reflect the truth of that unconditional love.

I have seen parents stand by their children in some of the most uncomfortable and unfortunate situations. I have seen the love and prayers of a parent be the only hope that a child held on to when everyone else had given up on them. I have seen parents who have sacrificed their own dreams for the dreams of their children. I have seen quiet, passive parents come out like a roaring lion when one of their cubs are threatened. I have seen parents on their knees, crying out to God to save their child from heading down a path that will lead to nothing but pain and consequences. I have seen parents go without so that their kids were provided for. And I have seen parents disrespected by these same kids, yet they still have an unfathomable love for them.

19

Parents have been accused of everything but loving their children because we live in a world that has defined love by "doing for me, agreeing with me, and allowing me." A minister friend once said, "Love is not the absence of truth." What a powerful statement. I didn't understand the struggle, sacrifice, joy, fear, discipline, and love of my parents until I became one.

Growing up, I so struggled with not feeling special and loved by my mom. I accused and convicted her of crimes that I felt she committed against me, not realizing that my mom had lived longer than me, so she recognized the red flags, detour signs, toxic thinking, and do-not-enter signs that I couldn't see. She tried by any means necessary to stop me from going down a path of destruction, and her wisdom was often received as criticism because of her delivery—but what if that was the only way she knew how to reach out and grab me before I fell into a lifestyle that she dreaded? I never even considered that maybe the things I expected from my parents they had never received as children.

Perception is a devourer of truth. It blinds us to a greater reality. We're moved by what we see and hear, never taking the time to really understand and look beyond our emotions. Perspective is everything. I allowed society, my friends, social media, reality TV shows, and *Lifetime* movies to influence me to view my mom as my enemy. I filtered her actions through these lenses, and it caused me years of pain, anger, unforgiveness, and pity.

Steve Jobs once said, "You can never connect the dots looking forward; you can only connect them looking backward. So you have to trust that the dots will somehow connect in your future."[3] That's a true statement indeed. Now that I am older, more mature, and a parent, I see my parents, especially my mom, through much clearer lenses.

My mom was the youngest of three siblings and the only girl. Her mother, whom I know little about other than she was a smart, kind, and beautiful woman, died from tuberculosis when my mother was three years of age. Due to this illness, my grandmother had been told that she probably shouldn't have any more children, but she was already pregnant with my mom. The doctors suggested terminating the pregnancy, but my grandmother refused and ended up giving birth to my mother in a tuberculosis institution. She deemed my mom worthy of life! Unfortunately, my grandmother never came home from that institution and my mom never really knew the woman who sacrificed her life for hers.

Losing her mom, whether she realized it or not, altered my mom's life. A part of her would always be missing, though she never realized what it was. When God began to enlighten my heart and remove the scales from my eyes, I was able to see something I had never seen before: My mom never knew the woman who spoke to her from the moment of her conception, the woman who had dreams for her before she ever came into this world, and the woman who would have encouraged her and reminded her of how beautiful she was when the world would tell her otherwise. She never knew the woman who held her and prayed over her as a baby. She could not remember her mother's voice to help guide her through her first heartbreak or give her the much-needed wisdom to make it through her teenage years. Her mom would never see her graduate, get married, or have children.

21

I often wonder how different her life would have been had she not lost her mom at such a young age and, moreover, how different my life would have been.

My mom had me at the age of twenty, a time when many people are still trying to figure out who they are. She had to determine her identity without the one person who deemed her worthy—without the person who carried her for nine months and knew her best. Twenty is also an age when people are trying to live their lives. Try doing that with a two-year-old and another child on the way. She was unwed, unequipped, and with no real parental guidance. Try building something with no tools, no clue, and no instructions. My mom had no real tools in her parenting tool belt. She wanted to be the hero in my and my sister's lives but had no power or cape to soar higher than her own experiences.

Looking back, I can see how hard it must have been to have a child who reminds you so much of yourself and to wonder if that child will make the same mistakes. You try to build a wall of protection around them without any knowledge of how to do that. I didn't see it that way. I felt like I was in a prison and my mom was the cruel warden, ridiculing everything I did. I felt that she couldn't stand me, that she loved my older sister more than me, that I could do nothing right in her eyes, and that some of the words she spoke, maybe out of anger, when I did something she didn't approve of, proved how much she didn't like me.

With new lenses, I can now see the full picture from a higher vantage point. My mom worked hard for us, even cleaning the bathrooms where she worked for extra money. She also taught us how to be independent and (in her own crazy way) that family was everything, no matter what we might go through. And she taught us to respect ourselves and our elders by snatching us up, popping us in our mouths, or whipping our behinds. It was not child abuse back then, or maybe it was, and we didn't know it.

I'm the woman I am today because of the woman who raised me. She isn't perfect, but she is the woman God chose to bring me into this world. Whatever mistakes she made, they were just that—mistakes. I'm a mom now and have made so many mistakes trying to raise my children. Where there is control, there is fear! I felt like my mom controlled every little thing I did. Not trusting me was her way of punishing me for being me, but the reality is she was afraid.

My kids have shared, in their own way, things that I've done because I too was missing some tools in my parenting tool belt. Yet I've been so blessed in my journey to have some amazing women who became my spiritual moms. They helped me heal, forgive, and mature. They also gave me some great tools. I made no excuses for the things I unintentionally did that may have hurt my kids, but rather offered understanding and asked for forgiveness instead. I see that even though all parents want to do is protect, teach, guide, and love their children with all their heart, they can find themselves hurting them in ways that they never imagined or intended.

I want my girls to look back through lenses of understanding, knowing that everything I did as a mom I did for them. I also pray that my mom realizes that she is an amazing mom, and that God wants to give her His cape so that she can fly, understanding that her latter years can and will be greater. I love my mom with all my heart, and I am truly grateful for every sacrifice she made for my sister and me.

Equally important is how I viewed my dad. I will start off by saying that I'm a daddy's girl and I love my daddy! To me, he is a simple man, always teaching us through his actions and not his words. He worked hard for his family, rested and partied some weekends, spoke his truth, and liked things his way. My dad had a calm demeanor when dealing with us kids, but we knew when he was serious. My dad also has a crazy sense of humor. He would hide in the house, and when we came home from school, he would wait until we got good and comfortable, then jump out and scare the living crap out of us.

He is also a storyteller. Maybe that's where my storytelling gift comes from. He would tell these crazy stories in such a convincing way that it took us a few days of questioning the stories before we realized he made them up. I think the attribute I admire most about my dad is that he woke up early to go to work to provide for his family. It wasn't even a question for me whether a man should work. My dad never really said much to me about dating and relationships, yet he would drop little nuggets of wisdom regarding what a man should be doing. He also believed there were certain things we had to learn for ourselves.

Now did I need my dad to be more involved, especially when it came to dating? Yes indeed. I needed him because sometimes he didn't know about something until it came knocking at his front door, so to speak, and I could no longer hide it.

One incident was when my high-school boyfriend at the time thought I was cheating on him, because I told him I didn't want to be with him anymore. He seemed like a great guy when we started dating in high school, but then he began to change. He joined a gang and became controlling and was starting to get physical with me. This time he snatched my house keys from my hand, broke into my house, and stole all my belongings.

I was hiding at my cousin's house, but he found out where I was and began threatening me. I was so scared, I ended up calling my dad and was forced to tell him everything that happened. My dad went to where my boyfriend hung out, and I was terrified that one of the gang members would hurt him to try to protect my ex-boyfriend. To this day, I don't know what my dad said to him, but he got my keys back and my ex-boyfriend never tried to hit or threaten me again.

I was left questioning why was I with a guy who had the potential to treat me in such a way. The only teenage answer I could come up with was that in the beginning, he was kind and paid so much attention to me. I did not necessarily see anything beyond that. I felt important and wanted; I was looking for affirmation. This is where I needed my dad. I needed him to see what I didn't.

Recently, my dad shared with me that when I was a little girl, he and my mom both spoiled me rotten. He said that he would always tell me how beautiful and special I was. Unfortunately, during my teenage years, the enemy came in and literally stole the fond memories we'd shared. The world's voice was much louder, and even though I knew he considered me his baby girl, I needed to hear the words, "You are a princess, and I put you on a pedestal. You better not come down for no man. Keep your standards high and require a guy to rise up to them and be the type of man a princess deserves."

I wanted my dad to ask me what was going on with the guys I was dating, or really be involved in knowing what I was doing. I was good at hiding and pretending innocence, and I needed my dad to see beyond that and pick up on the clues. I needed him to see that my boyfriends reflected how I saw myself. I needed him to talk to me about how to deal with certain things about guys because I was so naive. I thought every guy was like him and didn't know how to recognize wolves in sheep clothing.

In interviewing my dad, I learned what had been deposited in him as a young boy—who taught him how to be a man, a father, and a husband. Growing up, he had to learn how to be his own man. I'd heard this statement before, but as my dad shared his journey with me, it provided a greater understanding. He learned to be a man even with his limited knowledge; he was writing his own book and created the table of contents along the way.

Even though my dad knew and loved his dad, he didn't grow up with him in the home because my grandparents divorced when he was five years of age. My grandpa then moved to Ohio. My dad was still very close to him and would visit him every summer until he was around thirteen or fourteen when, as a teenager, he stopped putting forth the effort to spend time with his dad.

I'm a firm believer that there are some strong single moms who have raised amazing men but there are still certain things a man needs to learn from a man. Would my dad's life have looked different had he lived with my grandpa—a man who, even though he had very little education, worked, built his own house, and took care of his family? And a man who once told my dad, "If I even dream that you disrespected me or your mom, I'm going to wake up and beat your ass." A man who showed him what working hard and being responsible looked like every time he visited. My dad needed the wisdom, discipline, and voice of his father.

In the same way, I needed affirmation and validation, the same affirmation and validation God gave His son Jesus when He was baptized. He called him "my son with whom I am well pleased." I believe it was God's design for the father to not only provide and protect, but also to affirm and validate. I don't believe my dad understood the impact his words carried for me as my father.

I've had the great pleasure of helping a lot of young women and men come to a place of wholeness, and I can tell you the root of most of their problems has been identity. So many of them came from a home without a father, and while that variable may be noticed, it's not addressed when we look at the issues in our society today, especially regarding young people.

I'm so grateful that I've had a dad who loves me unconditionally, and just like with my mom, I am who I am because of who he is. He's told me that the highlight of his life is being a dad! I'm glad he had the courage to write his own table of contents. Even though he didn't know the plot or book's ending, he learned how to live by faith.

As we were finishing up the interview, my dad told me another one of his stories. I don't know if it's true, but I know his resolve was. He stated that he was drinking one day and must have had too much, because he thought he was going to die. He said in that moment, all he could think of was to make sure my auntie told us—his children—that he loved us and that he hoped he made us proud. That's my dad, my hero! He will never have to ask that question because I want to boldly say, "Yes, you make us proud."

They say when the student is ready, the teacher will come. There are pivotal times in our lives when we're ready to receive truth, wisdom, and guidance, and ready to see the things that we were blind to. We were blind because we just weren't ready to make a hard decision or see a bad choice. We weren't ready to let people go, forgive, and heal. We all have blinders—it's nothing to be ashamed of—but it's something that each of us needs to be aware of, because it can cost us our life.

Take a car, for instance. Every car has a rearview mirror and a side mirror, so the driver can see what's coming up behind and on the side, yet new drivers are always taught to turn around and look over their shoulder when changing lanes or backing up, because the mirrors have blind spots.

I see things clearer now that I've accepted that there's more to the story than just the beginning and the end. There are events, tragedies, plots, and climaxes that could have changed the beginning, thereby altering the ending. That's why by the end of a story, we usually have a different view of the characters.

Perspective is everything.

# Original

I STRUGGLED FOR A long time with being an original, struggled to understand that who I am is not dependent on the opinions and views of man. What comes to mind when one thinks of being an original? Some say authentic, pioneer, forerunner, creator of the unknown—of something never seen or done before. Well, I say it's the beginning of self, yet the sad reality is that most people will spend their entire life without ever knowing their true identity. We never look beyond the surface of what we see in the mirror. Never find the courage to turn off the lights, to be forced to feel, search, and uncover the greatness that darkness unconsciously tries to hide. There was a false need to be everything but me. Therefore, I tried repeatedly to uproot this unwanted seed.

I struggled to chisel through the manmade rocks of insecurities, as I continued to argue with self, barricading and muffling out the sound of my own voice, because I did not want to face the undetected truth that I was simply AFRAID.

And like a sponge, my fears absorbed the bacteria of my reality, the reality that we live in a world that gives more leniency to evil than to good, a world where we compromise ourselves and our integrity way more than we should, a world that talks about unity but we can't even speak to our neighbors in our own community. A world that cares more about being seen than being heard, a world where people are much quicker to tear you down than to take a moment to speak a word of encouragement that could build you up. A world that has created a platform for fake reality shows and Facebook gossip that everyone knows ... constantly giving off the message that it's all about the titles, the shape of our bodies, the clothes we wear, and all the materialistic things like the cars, the houses, and the bling.

See, we are so eager to climb the ladder to success instead of staying on the ground floor by being ourselves, creating our own stage to bring something new and powerful to this present age. Listen, when we begin to pull back the layers of excuses, we simply find ourselves, because where there is a will there's a way, and I don't know what anyone else calls it, but I call it faith.

So when I think about this world's condition, I can better understand my purpose and my mission—to give the world what God has given me to bring about a change and make a difference.

For instance, Ruby Bridges—a little black girl with the courage to challenge a segregated world. She became a part of history, she attempted to do something that had never been done, standing alone risking death amid the eyes of judgment of her peers. Rejected because of the color of her skin and because she wanted the opportunity of an equal education, and to be herself and be accepted.

That's why I can no longer adjust myself until there is nothing of me left.

This mission I won't abort, but I choose to give birth to my self-worth, and I will watch it grow, evolve into what it was destined to be, and I will take full responsibility to feed it with passion, protect it with authenticity, invest in its future with hard work and faith, and during the times that I don't know what to do, I will fall on my knees and pray, and one day I will be a proud mother of destiny.

See, the sound that I bring has never been heard, the path that I walk hasn't been traveled, and the gifts that I bring have never been seen, because just like you, I'm not your average human being.

My words might not be poetic and smooth, but I have the words that can heal many wounds, words that reveal the reality of what is real. My thoughts are my own, and my consequences as well as my rewards are from seeds I myself have sown.

My copyright is through Jesus Christ, and if the approval of man was the key to success, then I would always find myself looking out and never in, and find myself becoming less.

That's why I no longer show up to perform so that through applauses my gifts and talents can be affirmed, even though they are always greatly appreciated. It is not through man I will be validated, because I've come to find out that insecurity is our greatest enemy; its strategy is to get you and me to renounce our true identity. If you never find out who you were meant to be, this fact will ultimately destroy you mentally, because everyone knows the mind is a powerful thing.

So, I don't know about you, but there will be no more suicide attempts on my purpose or my gifts, because the greatest demonstration of freedom is being one's self.

Your arrival does not mean my departure. Listen, there is enough room on this plane heading to success, and everyone can have his or her own seat because every seat belongs to self. We all have our own DNA...Divine Natural Ability to be all that God uniquely created us to be.

So if I never get any snaps, I will be the one the singer, Ledisi, is waiting for to stand up and clap for myself, because I will undeniably always be an original and I will never die a copy of somebody you never knew.

———————•  •———————

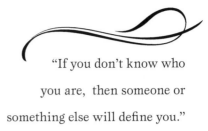

"If you don't know who

you are, then someone or

something else will define you."

—*Tiffany James*

# CHAPTER THREE

# It's Time to Stop Pretending

I'll take Identity for 500, Alex. The big *Jeopardy* question is "Who am I?"—the universal question gnawing at the soul of every human being, and the true answer is what satisfies the soul.

> *"When you know who you are, then you know what you can accomplish. When you know what you can accomplish, then you know what you need in order to do so."* —*Anonymous*

See, it's never about what you do, but who you are. What you do flows from a place of being. It's so sad that it took me almost forty-one years to figure this out. Think about it for a minute.

From a young age, we're pushed to get the best grades, to speak a certain way, to strive to look a certain way, and to have a certain body type (my desired body type was the old Coca-Cola bottle, and I felt like I came up short since I had no boobs).

We're forced to participate in sports because it's supposed to create character through healthy competition, and we're to strive to do it all: be homecoming king or queen, graduate as valedictorian, attend a prestigious college, get married, have two kids (girl and boy, twins would be perfect), buy a big house with a maid, wear nothing but name brand clothes, and drive a top-of-the-line car. The Cosby family came close, so hey, it must be the life.

So we already have some type of false perception of what the perfect life looks like from a young age. This perception becomes a dark tomb where we just exist and never really live, where we look at everything outside ourselves to define who we are. We start allowing these things to devalue us if we don't possess them. All these things are constantly screaming, "You do not measure up!" We're forced to conform to a system that existed before our time, and we don't even know who deemed it as the universal way to be.

In trying to conform, we find ourselves feeling like we aren't good enough, aren't smart enough, aren't handsome or beautiful enough, or are too big or too small. We find ourselves always trying to reinvent the wheel, as if the original version of ourselves wasn't perfect. We start to pretend by becoming someone that we aren't and doing things that are contrary to our original design.

Somewhere in our lives, we experience an incident—a lie, a disappointment, a loss, or a person—that causes us to abandon who we are and who we were created to be. Yes, there was an upside-down event. It was as if our personality was altered in an instant. Something or someone made us believe that living in the Land of I am was impossible, that being ourselves was not enough. We went from being to doing, from purposed to pretending, from thriving to striving. We literally became a counterfeit and didn't even realize it.

I am a big kid at heart, and I live in a world where the characters on the TV screen and in movies teach me valuable lessons. For example, the movie *The Lion King* taught me by showing how Simba's life spiraled out of control. I saw Simba go from purposed to pretending.

The movie starts off with Simba being presented, honored, blessed, and praised for who he is predestined to be. (I need you to really catch that one—he is celebrated as if he has already succeeded as king because it is his birthright.) As a young cub, Simba is very curious, energetic, bold, courageous, and hard-headed. Yet young Simba has a great mentor, his father, who is grooming him to not only be a king, but a great king. He is teaching Simba valuable lessons, so he can govern his kingdom well.

Later in the movie, a group of hyenas come after him and his friend. Simba, despite his small size and being outnumbered, shows great courage. He has a natural instinct to protect. Being king is all he knows.

I love the part when Simba begins to sing about how he can't wait to be king. Do you remember when you were a young Simba and felt like you could conquer the world? You were singing your own anthem: "Oh, I just can't wait to be (fill in the blank)."

For me, my song was constantly changing because I wanted to be everything. I couldn't wait to be queen of dance for a famous R&B singer. I couldn't wait to be the highest-paid sharpshooter prosecutor in the courtroom, with my tight black pencil skirt and fitted white blouse, not to mention black pumps and hair pulled straight back because, like Matlock, I meant business. I couldn't wait to be motivational speaker. And I couldn't wait to be queen of my own talk show.

Somewhere along the way, like Simba, I lost my voice. Someone or something caused me to change the words to my anthem. Simba is so naive that he doesn't realize that he has an enemy. Not everyone is celebrating who he is destined to become. He allows a lie told by his uncle, Scar, to steal his anthem. (It really hurts when it's family who does that.) Scar recruits the hyenas and concocts a plan to kill not only Simba's father, Mufasa, but also the royal heir.

He places Simba on a rock, lies to him about a special time with his father, and leaves him there to be trampled by a stampede. Then Scar calls out to Mufasa to rescue his son, but all along Scar isn't expecting either to live. Simba does survive, however, and we see the young, now-brokenhearted Simba lying under his father's lifeless body. (Who does that to a child? Well, it happens more than we realize. There are many kids—you might be one—who are living with the guilt of something that they had no control over.)

The voice of guilt and shame then speaks to Simba, making him feel like a failure and a mistake, not a king. He runs away from his kingdom, his dream, and his birthright, while his anthem fades into the wind as he heads into the wilderness—into the land of false perception.

He is introduced to two of the funniest, kindest, and most unusual animals, Pumbaa and Timon. Simba is now a confused, scared, angry, and hurt little cub with no sense of purpose anymore. Pumbaa and Timon become his newfound friends. They take him under their wings and give him a new anthem: "*Hakuna Matata*," which means "no worries for the rest of your days."

They tell Simba when the world turns its back on you, you turn your back on it. This mentality is a contradiction to who he was. We see Simba start taking on this new yet false identity, and he now seems happy, as if he really is living the life (a problem-free life, no less). This might have been true, but there is one problem: Simba was born to be king.

Now we see the king of the jungle eating bugs, getting fat, and singing nursery rhymes. It sounds absurd, yet it's his new norm. Simba experiences his own upside-down event; he might have been comfortable and maybe even happy, but he is not king—and there is a knowing within Simba that will not relent.

Simba, no longer a cub but now a lion, is lying down one night, looking at the sky, when he remembers his dad's wisdom that the great kings of the past will always be there to guide him. You too can try to silence the voice of your purpose within you, but you will fail miserably. It'll keep calling you until the day you close your eyes and take your last breath. Simba had developed a false perception of himself, and that perception became his false reality. He accepted it until his past catches up to him, reminding him of who he is.

My favorite part is when the monkey, who blessed Simba when he was first presented to the kingdom to be the next heir, finds out that Simba is alive and goes after him. He lures Simba to the water by saying that Mufasa is still alive, and Simba, in hopes of seeing his father, follows. The monkey instructs Simba to look into the water, but when he looks, he only sees his own reflection and his father is nowhere to be found. The monkey tells him to look harder, and when he does, he sees the reflection of his father. He finally sees who he is! His legacy is staring right back at him.

He remembers he was born to be king, that it wasn't just a song but also his birthright. He goes back to take his rightful place, even though that means he will have to face his past. When he returns, Simba realizes the impact of his decision to run away from who he was created to be. His kingdom has been reduced to a wasteland under the rule of his uncle, Scar.

Yes, who you were created to be is intertwined with a purpose, and that purpose is bigger than you. When you shrink back, something is reduced to a wasteland because it's waiting on you to water it with what is needed for it to thrive. There are people in bondage, like Simba's family, and you are the one God has chosen to challenge and defeat the enemy that stole their freedom.

Simba didn't do anything special to prepare to defeat his uncle and take back rule over his lands, and sometimes you don't have time to make sure you have it all together before you decide to face your past, defeat the enemy and his lies, and take your rightful place. Sometimes you just have to believe! You must trust what has been spoken over your life; it's called moving out in faith. Like with Simba, God has placed people in our lives to remind us who we are. We must find the courage to believe it even when we ourselves can't see it.

I will sum up the movie and this chapter by saying that Simba found the courage to face his past, he believed what the monkey (the voice of wisdom and truth) spoke to him, and he believed what he knew in his heart to be true even though he had been too afraid to embrace it. He took his rightful place as king, he restored his kingdom, and at the end we see that Simba also gets his voice back as he lets out the most powerful roar with the authority of a king. He no longer has to sing his anthem because he learned how to live in his truth—he was always a king.

You can no longer pretend! Ask yourself, *How long will I hide? How long will I allow circumstances to change the words to my song? How long will I eat bugs? How long will I settle for being comfortable when I am supposed to be ruling?* It's time for you to confront whatever it is that caused you to run or shrink back from your purpose. It's time for you to find your voice. Remember, anything that is lost can be found. Take your rightful place!

It's time for you to rule again.

## Greatness

GREATNESS UNRECOGNIZED IS A seed of potential. Out of the hollowness of your soul, it calls out to you. It will not be denied and can no longer be confined; it is absolute. Greatness never apologizes, it is comfortable looking back, and it is never afraid to press forward. It is not a shadow of what is to come, but a reflection of what already is. It's never blind to the truth but is constantly challenged by it. Greatness is never to be boxed in by the walls of expectations.

The depths of your disconnect to greatness show the level of your fear, causing you to deny yourself each time.

You may get stuck while searching for a path to greatness through the crevasses of the soul, but never give up your quest, because greatness hungers for the purpose it was meant to fulfill. Every time you tap into your purpose, you tap into greatness. When the sun rises, it shows its greatness; when it sets, it shows its greatness because it knows its purpose. Greatness may be nervous, maybe even a little unsure, but it is never afraid to look you in the eye, because greatness honors greatness. It shuts out the doubters, binds the excuses, and is never hindered by rejection, but is empowered by it.

Greatness is patient as well as impatient. It does not complain but does what is needed to bring about change. We all have this innate desire to be something better than our current self. You must understand it's because we were created with the ability to enhance. Desiring to be more does not mean anything is wrong with who you are. You are enough! Remember, greatness is a seed, and there is nothing wrong with a seed. It has an innate ability to become. Greatness is nothing to strive for or even something to obtain, because it is a state of being. Greatness is always reinventing itself. A beautiful unveiling of truth!

It encourages everyone, it respects everyone, and it makes room for others.

Greatness is an exhilarating journey that we are all on!

CHAPTER FOUR

# Greatness Is Learning How to Reign in Purpose

I was born with the authority to decree my destiny. I was born to rule in the Land of I am. It is my voice that everything in the land must submit to. When there is tragedy in the land, it's my voice that carries the authority that will determine how the land survives. It's my strength that will rebuild the ruins.

I don't follow the rules of the world. I once heard a saying that rules are meant to be broken. If that's the case, I get an A+, because I don't play by the rules anymore. I live by the standards that God and I have laid as my foundation.

I have some questions that I want you to ponder: What if every child was raised as royalty? What if every child was taught, from the time they were born, that they were special and born to rule? I want to let you in on a truth: You are not chosen to be royalty by some special trait or ability you possess; you are actually born into royalty—it's in your blood.

Now some of you might say my bloodline is far from royal, but if we could trace our lines back to the beginning, we would see that we're all part of a royal bloodline, which is the bloodline of Christ. Until you recognize this truth and understand who you are in Him, you will always find yourselves questioning who you are. But once you realize you're royalty, you'll see that you can do all things through Christ, who is your strength, your voice, your guide, your everything!

Okay, I feel an inspirational moment coming on. Let's grab a little bit more of the first piece, "I Didn't Know My Own Strength," from chapter one:

SOMEHOW, I WAS ABLE to see that greater is He that is in me—that truth canceled out all the lies, and out of the ashes and the dust I began to arise a new creation despite the planning of my demise. I was still standing, and no matter what it looked like, I did not lose, for God gave me a second chance, providing me the power to choose.

And I chose courage instead of fear, hope so that I can heal. I chose sunshine instead of sorrow, I chose to live for today and allow God to worry about my tomorrow. See when I look back over my life, even when others walked away, He never left my side. That's why I choose life instead of death, that's why I choose to walk away rather than lose myself in a situation because I stayed. And, most importantly, I choose to change.

See, there is nothing wrong with change if you're headed in the right direction, and today I'm headed in the direction of forward movement and positive thinking, seizing every moment and savoring every minute. I'm no longer dependent on what I see in front of me or what this world feels like it has to offer me; I am back on a journey toward my divine destiny, and I hear different voices calling out to me.

Voices of greater leaders who have gone before, such as Marianne Williamson, who reminds me that "my deepest fear is not that I am inadequate, but that I am powerful beyond measure—that it was my light, never my darkness, that frightened me. I began to question myself ... who am I to be gifted, talented, phenomenal? Actually, who am I not to be? I am a child of God, and my playing small does not serve the world, and there is nothing enlightened about me shrinking so that others won't feel insecure.

I was born to manifest the glory of God in me, and it's not for some of us but for each and every last one of us, and as we let our light shine, we give others permission to do the same. As we are liberated by our own fears, our very presence liberates others,"[4] so I now stand before you, liberated and free to tell my story like so many that have gone before me. How through it all—the pain, the hurt, the rejection, the lies, the betrayal, and the disappointment—I found my strength, and it was in God all along.

I am a seed of purpose. I was created on purpose for a purpose, and fulfilling that purpose is what greatness really is. A seed can only produce its own kind. You too are a seed of purpose, so you can't do anything but produce greatness. It's not what you do; it's who you are. You are a seed of greatness because you come from greatness. You are a beautiful representation of God in the earthly realm, and when you shrink back or try to become someone else, then there is a part of Him that is not being seen, and there is a part of you that you will never really know.

Yes, the God of all creation chose you to represent a part of Him in the earthly realm. He placed the ability to be great inside you. Did you know that you were born with seeds of greatness? Those seeds are called potential. According to Dictionary.com, *potential* is defined as "having or showing the capacity to become or develop into something in the future."[5] This means that once you come into the fullness of that potential, it ceases to be potential and becomes purpose. A purpose is the reason for which something exists or is done, made, or used. In a way, your potential helps you fulfill your purpose, and this means you lack nothing.

When a seed dies, it literally dies to itself so that it can grow. You can dig up a plant, but you will not find that seed; it ceases to be a seed so that the plant can grow, mature, and live. In the same way, you never cease to possess those natural abilities; they just mature into something greater in you. Yes, you are a garden with so much potential (ability) to become who you were created to be.

If you have ever had a garden, then you know that you must plant your seeds in good soil, water them, tend to them, and protect them, so that one day you will have the awesome opportunity to see the array of beautiful fruit, vegetables, and flowers that stand on their own but also complement and complete each other. Waiting for that seed to blossom can be a little frustrating, and I know you can be disappointed when it looks like that seed isn't growing in the season you wanted it to or the way you wanted it to grow, but that seed has the potential to be something beautiful.

I was raised to believe that I was born into circumstances that dictated mediocrity. I was not born of what the world would define as royalty. I was born and raised under the false pretense that I was ordinary—of no special quality or of any real importance. Society wanted me to believe that because of my past and being born into a family that hadn't done any great exploits in their eyes, that my lot in life was simply to survive. I believed that I had absolutely no power to change my life, and that I should be grateful that I had made it thus far—grateful that I at least made it to average.

I'm here to tell you that survival was my starting line, not my finish line. The world wanted me to accept that I was just another undistinguished, everyday run-of-the-mill person.

Now don't forget my piece "I Didn't Know My Own Strength." I always knew deep inside that I was far from average. There was a voice crying out in the wilderness, and I recognized the voice; it was the voice of purpose. It was the voices of kings and queens living in their own Land of I am telling me how they discovered it. I think I was fearful because everything was screaming, "Shut up!" and "Give up!" but at the same time, the voice of courage was saying, "Keep going. Don't give up, because there is something in you that you haven't yet explored and discovered."

I didn't know where to start, but I heard an old proverb: "A wise man looks to his ancestors, not to mimic them but to learn from them." There is so much we can learn from those who have gone before us and learned how to walk in their God-given authority to be who they were created to be. We can understand that their great exploits, sacrifices, and self-discovery are more than just history, but elements of who they are, who we are, and how we all identify ourselves in a world that tries to downplay our existence.

Those who have gone before us learned that they were created for a purpose, never realizing that one day they would be considered "great" by doing so. We should always stand on our feet with our heads held high, because we stand upon the shoulders of those who have cultivated what it means to reign in greatness.

Many people have inspired me on my journey to self-acceptance, teaching me that being great is part of my inheritance. One in particular is Sidney Poitier. I can't quite remember why or how I found out about his book *The Measure of a Man*, but it encouraged me to peel off the labels that I allowed others to put on me. I purchased the audio book and fell in love with this man.

He had an inner strength that I couldn't explain, and a tenacious boldness to stand up for what he believed. He fought to be seen for who he was and not as someone else saw him. If you've never read his book, after you finish this one, get the audio version. After listening to Sydney every day on my way to work, I became a little obsessed and purchased every one of his movies—*Lilies of the Field*; *Guess Who's Coming to Dinner*; *To Sir, with Love*; *A Patch of Blue*; and *The Defiant Ones*.

I believe Sidney always lived in the Land of I am. I recall listening to him tell the story of how he was looking for a job as a dishwasher and could not find one, but while looking through the newspaper, he came across an ad for the American Negro Theater. There was nothing he didn't believe he could do, so he went to audition.

Because of Sydney's thick Caribbean accent, the man who placed the ad tried to decide for him that he was not meant to be an actor, but a dishwasher. Sidney recalls that was the day his life changed. He wondered how the man knew he was a dishwasher since he had never said he was. From that day forward, Sydney was determined to prove that man wrong. Who was this man to come into his land and try to rule who he was destined to be?

How many times have people tried to tell you who you should be or what you should be doing—or what you can and cannot do? How many times have we partnered with other people's opinions of us because we didn't have the confidence or the courage to believe in ourselves, speak up, and listen to the inner voice screaming, "That's not who you are!"? We live in a world where we care more about being accepted than about being ourselves. We care more about fitting in than ruling.

What if Sidney had walked away, agreeing with another man's perception of him? What if he would have conformed to the image of an opinion? Being a dishwasher was not who he was, but what he did at the time, and he always knew that he was capable of more.

Like Sidney, you'll have to prepare yourself and hone in on your gifts; that's called being a good steward of what God has given you. Some of us don't want to do anything. We believe God is a genie in a bottle. We rub our hands together, voice our desires, and expect our three wishes will instantly be granted. No, He is a God of purpose, and the reality is that you must take care of anything you have been given.

For a garden to grow, it must be tended. You can't just plant the seeds and never water them. You must water the garden, make sure the soil is good, remove the weeds, and do whatever else a good gardener does (I wouldn't know because I don't do gardens!). But I know and respect the process.

Sidney did the work. He watered the seeds of his potential with knowledge. He taught himself how to read with the help of a waiter where he worked and by listening to the radio broadcasting station to improve his speaking. In addition, he had the courage and the humility to go back to the theater and take an unpaid job as a janitor in order to get free acting lessons. Do you remember that Serenity Prayer? "God grant me the *serenity* to accept the things I cannot change, the *courage* to change the things I can, and the *wisdom* to know the difference"? Sidney couldn't change that he was black, he couldn't change that he was born in what people would call poverty, he couldn't change his thick accent, and he couldn't change the way people viewed him. Yet he had the courage to try new things and challenge a society that stated he was only good enough to wash dishes. He had the courage to learn how to read, to try again, and to dream big.

I believe he had wisdom to know the difference, and that's why he's considered a great legend who broke barriers that seemed to be unbreakable. As he put it, "I am the me I choose to be."[6]

Greatness is always asking you to rule.

A few years back, I attended a Tyler Perry play for the first time. There at the Paramount in Oakland, California, I started to cry as the play unfolded. At the time, I wasn't quite sure why endless tears were streaming down my cheeks during a play that was supposed to make me laugh. I tried to hold back the tears, but they burned within me. I couldn't comprehend my irrational behavior for weeks, months, and even years afterward. What was a sista going through? Was there a hole in my soul—a longing for something that I couldn't fathom? I had no gauge to describe the longing that tortured me from that day forward.

Two years after seeing the play and having a mini nervous breakdown, my husband took me to the Concord Pavilion to see Mary J. Blige in concert (I *love* her!). Her songs and testimony pulled me out of some pretty deep ditches in my young adult years, so you can understand why I was so excited to be sitting only a few feet from a woman who became my lyrical best friend even though she didn't know it.

As the concert began, I felt like a little kid seeing Mickey Mouse at Disneyland for the first time. After two songs, she told a little of her testimony before going into another song, and all of a sudden out of the depths of my soul, I began to weep and once again found myself trying (but failing miserably) to keep my tears from falling. I thought to myself, *No one will know why I'm crying, including myself.* I figured they would chalk it up to me being sentimental after hearing her testimony. So I let the tears flow, and to my surprise they began to speak to me and I realized they had been trying to all along.

This irrational crying episode was the same as the one I had two years earlier while watching the Tyler Perry play. The only difference was that this time I was ready to listen. My tears began to water the seeds of greatness lying dormant within.

See, greatness recognizes greatness, and it was asking me why I was silent. Tyler Perry, Mary J. Blige, Steve Harvey, Oprah, Sidney Poitier, and many others had learned a powerful secret: they learned how to be! They allowed the message of their abilities to speak to the world in its own language with unrestricted access, crossing over into the hearts of all of mankind. They were challenging me to do the same. No more excuses or fear!

Like Indiana Jones, I found myself drawn to the unknown, and I knew it would appear to be an impossible, long, adventurous, risky, and downright crazy expedition. (This was about ten years ago.) I had stumbled onto something valuable, and I knew the enemy of nonconformity would be after me. Yet this time I was encouraged, empowered, courageous, and ready to rule. I was learning how to be my true authentic self, and the seeds of my potential were blooming; I was walking in my greatness.

I always had a natural ability as an encourager; it was intricately woven into who I was, and I realized there was a purpose within my ability. What you conquer, you have authority over. This was the beginning of defeating the enemy of my soul. I was taking my rightful place and learning how to rule, and I felt compelled to break the shackles of lies off others. It was time to train others to find and take back their voice—and not with voice articulation. This was about helping others make their thumbprint on the world. I wanted to teach them how to be great by being and embracing their true authentic self, because when you discover this, then you discover greatness.

Merriam-Webster states that *greatness* is "exceptionally high quality, outstanding, distinction."[7] It refers to individuals who possess a natural ability to be better than all others. Greatness is an acquisition of status by the people who have contributed to an organization, group, or purpose that is greater than themselves. I have one problem with this definition: it disqualifies many by stating their natural ability must be better than *all* others.

If it's a natural ability, then it's not about being better, but being unique in what you were created to do. The moment we begin to compare ourselves is the moment we start to trust our perception and not our Creator. Many people disqualify themselves from being great because they're defining it based off their ability or inability to be better than someone else.

I want you to realize that you set the standard of greatness every time you're being the best version of yourself. Succeeding at being who you were created to be, is the true definition of greatness. Yes, there will be some struggles, sacrifices, disappointments, losses, and even some critics, but that can't stop you. God will never give you more than you are able to handle with His help; He will use every situation to work for good. In addition, you'll be learning how to walk in the authority given to you to fulfill your purpose.

So allow your abilities to open up so that they can be the parachute that takes you on a new and unexpected adventure, exploring the endless possibilities, the fresh air of freedom, with no boundaries and no borders, where everything is silenced but the wind of opportunity. Nike stated it best: "Greatness is a choice."[8] So choose today to believe in yourself and reign in greatness.

The first responsibility in walking into your greatness is believing you can.

## Dreams & Visions

As CRAZY AS IT may seem, I couldn't even imagine making it this far without my dreams. They've been my best friend, forever loyal to me. Always anxious to show me the most unbelievable things, but patient enough to wait until the night was quiet and the air was still.

Waiting until I was comfortable enough to be confronted with the things they knew I was capable of becoming, but too afraid to step out on in the light. Yes … my dreams became my courage. They shielded my insecurities, and they constantly pursued me because they knew I was chosen for destiny.

My dreams taught me so many important things, like to never try to live in anybody else's dream. They taught me as long as you continue to dream and believe in your dreams as much as they believe in you, everything you prayed for, longed for, and hoped for is capable of coming true. They taught me that this has been from before our time, all the way down through our spiritual bloodline.

See, our brother Joseph also had a dream of one day being a ruler or a king. A dream that lifted him up from the pit and stood by him within the walls of the prison cells, but Joseph made it because he held on to his dreams through it all. His dreams showed him the most unbelievable things, and we all know the Scripture, so you might as well say Joseph became that king.

Now you might say that was back in the Bible days, but there was another great man who had nothing but a dream—that one day all God's children would be treated equally and people of every color would one day be free at last, and we all know the history, so you know the dream of Martin Luther King Jr. has come to pass.

I too had a dream that I would be able to encourage, inspire, and bless people through what I speak—that the writings God imparted in me would create a unique legacy, and today I'm living this dream.

So, brothers and sisters, stretch your imagination, close your eyes so you can see the world, begin to dream, and, as my boy Tyler Perry always inspired me to do, dream a bigger dream. Dream until your dreams believe!

They'll be your biggest cheerleaders. They will comfort you, guide you, mold you, motivate you, and speak volumes to you. Don't you know your dreams will even write the vision for you? And if you have faith and just believe, your dreams will even become you.

So I'm going to leave you with a quote that recently freed my mind just a little bit more: "Work as if you don't need the money, love like your heart has never been broken, and dance as if no one in the room is watching."[9] I will add to it and say to dream as if your life depends on it, and live the vision for God Himself has pre-written for you.

And when you feel you don't have anything else, know that you have God and your visions, so continue to dream and live this life without limits, and when the mirror stares at you with words of defeat, saying you can't, I want you to be reminded of God's Word that states you can do all things, and stare back and say, "Yes, I can," and today find the courage to go as far as your dreams are willing to take you!

Chapter Five

# Lost Destiny, Redefined Purpose

P urpose is the reason for which something exists or is done, made, used, etc. I have a question for you: What if you were stolen from your land? Taken away from the place you called home—from the place you owned? The movie *Roots* makes my heart pound within my chest and my brain work overtime trying to comprehend what Africans who were brought to America endured.

They were stolen, ridiculed, beaten, masqueraded around like animals, separated from their family, treated with unimaginable cruelty, forced to live as slaves, and sold off like pieces of property, only to be used up until they died or were killed. Not to mention forced to watch their people die daily. Each one was nothing more than a commodity, no longer the owner of oneself.

What if the voice of your destiny was stolen from you, leaving you with no authority to speak the words that would carry the weight and break the chains of false purpose that were placed on you? It would be a nightmare that you keep waking up to each day, hoping that day will be the one when you have the power to defeat the evil villain, only to find out that the plot and the conclusion have already been written, and not in your favor.

There's a scene in *Roots* where Kunta Kinte, a young slave, is being brought to the plantation. Upon his arrival, he's given a new name by his white plantation owner, but he refuses to take on a name that is not his—or an identity that is false. His name, Kunta, carries purpose; it means to be awakened or to be aware.

Before being taken into slavery, he was aware of who he was created to be and what he would accomplish. Nevertheless, he is forced to take on a name that carries a totally different destiny, "Toby," which means "to serve." This means that Kunta Kinte, along with many others, was no longer the owner of his destiny. He is no longer free, but is now a slave with no rights, no history, no family, no purpose, and no real reason to live. He is forced to serve and cultivate another man's land.

Can you imagine living a life that is a lie designed to kill you? Can you imagine living every day with the knowledge that there is a greater purpose for your life but you have no rights to pursue it?

Today many people, young and old and from every nationality, are struggling with Toby syndrome. Society, music videos, talk shows, reality TV, magazines, finances, and materialistic possessions have somehow gained power over us. We've allowed these things to define us, while they take us farther and farther from the Land of I am.

We're trying to be true to ourselves as the voices of conformity, comparison, and competition are magnified, all while the whip of persuasion to be somebody else rips through the soul of your identity. We find ourselves in bondage to a false image that we keep bowing down to, but it's time to find the courage to leave everything behind, not consulting your master, and run toward freedom—toward the Land of I am.

In college, I was compelled to see a movie because it would give me much-needed extra credit in my African-American history class: *Twelve Years a Slave*. It's the true story of a talented violinist and well-to-do free African-American man from New York State named Solomon Northup, who was kidnapped and sold into slavery in the South. He was known and employed by many white plantation owners, and with this knowledge, two white men offered him employment as a musician in Washington, DC, but their plan all along was to steal his papers that proved he was born a free man and sell him to the slave pen.

I want you to imagine being in a place of total acceptance, walking in your purpose in spite of the circumstances surrounding you, only to make a decision that would alter the course of your destiny—a decision that would cost you your freedom involuntarily, and now you've had to fight twelve years (or even longer) to prove who you are. You find yourself spending years trying to prove to a perfect stranger that you were never who they branded you to be.

A couple of days after watching *Twelve Years a Slave*, I found myself lying on the floor, going through old photos from my past. In one picture, I had a smile on my face as I was surrounded by my high-school peers, people I allowed to have an unpaid position in defining who I was during that time. They showed up each time without fail, happy to tell me who they needed me to be or who they thought I should be. I let them dictate what my destiny would be by making choices that were contrary to who I was, and I'm sure I was not the only one. We had no grid for what it meant to walk in purpose, so many of us thought we were destined to do nothing but survive.

As I stared at the pictures, I noticed the gang signs being thrown up that we represented without a real cause, realizing now that our so-called gang signs represented our insecurities, loneliness, anger, and longing to belong. The senseless shootings, the meaningless handshakes, the gang colors—they were simply rooted in ignorance. We had no clue who we were.

Many of the young men were fatherless, wanting to be men but not having guidance from real men. These young boys were doomed to repeat the history of failure if they continued to believe the lie that there was nothing more to life than the five-block radius that we called our set, our territory, our turf. Many were willing to die without a cause, as if our lives were nothing more than feathers plucked off a duck. Life kept moving, tears eventually ceased until the next shooting, and our hope for something better in life grew narrower.

Young women fought over the same guy as if men were becoming extinct—which in our neighborhood on the South Side of Chicago, it appeared as though they were. I remember like it was yesterday, the last funeral I attended before saying that I had to get out of Chicago before the streets destroyed me.

My friend Author wasn't even eighteen years old when he was shot thirteen times. I couldn't believe that my neighborhood brother, who I had been laughing with earlier that day, was gone! He would never graduate and live out his full potential. This couldn't be what he was destined for. All of what he could have been was buried with him in the cold, hollow ground, as he was the victim of yet another senseless killing.

Author was a good kid with the ability to be great. I don't know how he or any of us got caught up in a gang, but I don't think we ever considered the possibility of dying. Like many others, he was young and wanted desperately to be heard, to be seen, and to belong, never realizing that the decisions we make today can impact our tomorrow.

The adults in our lives watching from the sidelines couldn't hear that our inner voices were screaming in fear that we were lost. I was one of those voices, and Author's funeral impacted me in such a way that I couldn't comprehend it at the time. I was unable to cope with the sad reality that life was no longer valuable to another human being. The truth was right in front of me—I was no longer numb to it—and it was that I was seventeen years old and attending more funerals than high-school dances.

Yes, something is wrong when girls no longer play with dolls because they're taking care of their own child at the age of seventeen. How many of them exchanged their double-dutch ropes for knives, or exchanged hopscotch for "dodge the bullet" because it was no longer safe to play in front of their houses? I knew something wasn't right when young men no longer played with monster trucks because a gun was their new fascination, except it wasn't a toy. I knew something was wrong when I saw my friends dying at the hands of another friend because of the neighborhood we lived in.

Our narrow perception of life made many believe they could never leave the hood. So, when it came to destiny, which was a word we didn't often hear when I was growing up, how could we believe anything other than what was right in front of us? Something was wrong, but was I the only one who saw it?

Broken homes, broken voices, broken hearts, broken innocence, and broken dreams equals a generation of brokenness. I was mad that a thief managed to make his way into our existence and snatch our innocence, dreams, identity, and purpose from us. I can't believe we voluntarily let him get away with it, as if we had no power to declare enough was enough.

Martin Luther King Jr. stated that "a riot is the language of the unheard."[10] The violence that I saw in my neighborhood—the violence we still read about or see on the news—is the voice of the broken, the wounded, the molested, the abandoned, the unloved, the disappointed, the frustrated, the hungry, the forgotten, the abused, the fatherless, the motherless, the unnamed, the impoverished, and the ridiculed. It cries out of unworthiness, pain, and evil; it is the voice of I am that has never been given the chance to be!

As I looked at the photos that captured a season of my life, I couldn't help but wonder what became of those I used to call my friends. Where were they now? Did they get sold off to another master? Or did they get their freedom papers and return to the Land of I am? Did they become who they were destined to be—doctors, lawyers, teachers, singers, gymnasts, engineers, psychologists, wives, husbands, mothers, fathers, mentors—or were they, like Kunta Kinte, Solomon Northup, and so many others, taken from their land, forced to live a life that a lie designed. A lie that said they were less-than.

Were they forced to live in a world system that was foreign to them, therefore making them feel powerless to fight for the truth flowing fiercely through their veins—that they were born free? Did they have the knowing within their being that this foreign place was not their destiny, but they thought they were so far gone from the Land of I am that they gave up? Did they stop their pursuit of freedom because they had no sense of direction, no resources, no way of knowing how to return?

Did hopelessness mock their current reality that they would never return? Or did they follow the hopes and dreams we shared before the world gave us boundaries and put the ocean of self-hatred in us to separate us from the Land of I am? Did the slave master of this society, or unfortunate circumstances, cripple their limitless imaginations to accomplish whatever they put their minds to?

My spirit became heavy with despair at the daunting truth of what was brewing underneath the surface of that very question, and that is that many never did. I wonder how many people are haunted by the thoughts of failure and disappointment that have had the power to cripple their spirits and enslave their minds. They say the wind cannot defeat a tree with strong roots, but what happens when there's no root system? What if there's nothing but disappointment and pain underneath the surface of a person? What if their beginning feels like their end?

Often, we want to ignore the variables of one's life. It's easy to pass judgment on a person because we've never had to live a day in their shoes. This is a sticky subject because there have been so many people who were able to overcome many obstacles in their life, so we try to put together a self-help formula for everyone, and when it fails, we blame the person. We make a quick judgment that they want to remain in the condition they're in. We believe that they were destined for failure. We actually believe that God made a creation in His image without a purpose.

Look, we all have a story and every story is different. Whether you were raised on the South Side of Chicago or in Beverly Hills, if the land is sick, if the land has been invaded and destroyed, if the land is dry and barren, if the land has been abandoned, then the land can't produce because the land needs healing! All those toxic variables must be uprooted before a new and healthy root system can be created. A seed will produce, but we don't know what seeds have been placed in the soul of a person.

I've seen successful people who have followed the five-step plan, so to speak, and have made great strides in their life— fame, awesome careers, nice cars, big houses, successful friends, and world travels—but there is a huge deficiency in their life. They have no real joy, nor are they ever really satisfied with anything. They have it all but live as if they don't. They carry a smile on the outside and the seed of bitterness inside. I know because I was one of them. While I wasn't bitter, I surely had no real joy. I was laughing on the outside while trying to mask the fear, unfulfillment, and unhappiness I felt within me.

There's always a root, so let's stop judging and start being a vessel of healing that brings about change in those whose destiny has been lost or stolen. Let's help them put their big-girl panties or big-boy boxers on and face the things that have choked out their purpose. It takes time to come from the darkness and into the light, from the pit of lies to the shore of truth. When people are really healed, they're truly free to be who they were created to be.

I want you to know that if something is lost, that means it exists and can be found. It may be buried under the lies of accusers, under the pain and disappointments, under the abuse, under the fear, under the insecurities, under the unfavorable circumstances, but it exists! As long as you have breath, there is still hope. Anything you were destined to do, if you believe and find courage instead of living in fear of the what-ifs and grab ahold of hope, you can heal and walk out your destiny. I believed and served hell notice that *survival* would be my starting line, not my finish line.

The sad part is that when we lose our identity, we also relinquish the authority given to us to fulfill our purpose. A lie is like cancer. It literally eats away at the cells of our identity. Most times, it sneaks in undetected and lies dormant, but it's busy in the darkness. If detected early, most of the time it's much easier to tackle and destroy. Sadly, like most cancer, it's often undetected and spreads, devouring us from the inside out.

If you're not living, then you're dying; it's like being buried alive. The lies have covered the seeds of greatness. They have hardened the soil, and nothing can grow. Can you imagine being buried alive? The very thought is suffocating.

I have some questions for you: If you had the opportunity to write your own eulogy, what would it say? What would your life speak to all those who gathered to say goodbye? Would your life inspire them to dream, to laugh, to believe that there is more, to embrace life with joy and expectation? What will your legacy be?

I challenge you to take a moment and answer these questions before moving to the next chapter.

## Bound Yet Free

IT'S BEEN SAID THAT a prison can only hold the body of man, but his mind has the power and right to be free. You get to choose your destiny even though your body is confined. No darkness can hide the light of destiny buried within the tomb of your very being. No bars can control the outcome of your tomorrow. Yes, it's another day within yet another day free. Free to make up in your mind that four walls, iron bars, the atmosphere of death, the mirrored reflection of hopeless and gloom, or any other authority that tries to control you be your reality.

Your mind controls your thoughts, your thoughts control your faith, your faith controls your trust, your trust controls your hope, your hope determines your decisions, your decisions open the doors to your freedom, and your freedom leads you to your destiny. Even though you are confined, your mind has the freedom to go wherever it chooses. You must guard your mind against the invasion of lies. Don't allow the mind-set of your atmosphere to manipulate you into believing that you are a mistake. Don't allow what you define as failure to become your attitude of confessing it's too late, for I am here to tell you that time isn't the determining factor of your fate. I know you might say, "But

how does one begin to survive this life hidden inside?"
I will say it again: only you can imprison your mind.

There is power in a moment and the moment is now. Yes, at the very moment your eyes embrace these words, these words can become your truth. Truth possess power, and you have the power within to be whatever you want to be, because right now you just became Free!

———————•  •———————

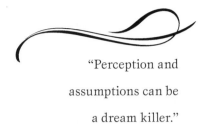

"Perception and
assumptions can be
a dream killer."

*—Tiffany James*

CHAPTER SIX

# Seeing Is Not Always Believing

*erception* is defined as "the ability to see, hear, or become aware of something through the senses."[11] It is a person's opinion of something or someone when they have no facts to back up their speculations. This creates a conflict when one's perception is inaccurate. Many of us have allowed other people's views of us to distort the truth of who we were created to be, and we succumbed to the pressure that perception puts on us to perform to everybody's expectation of us.

I struggled with this most of my life, always looking to others to tell me who I was and who I should be. I became addicted to other people's opinions of me because I needed to be accepted, always looking outward, never inward, to find out who I really was. It was like waiting on someone to come and give me permission to breathe—like I was always gasping for air. Who am I today? What is my purpose? Who can I be in the future? Am I pretty enough? Am I valuable and worthy? What makes me special? Will anyone ever love me?

What happens when no one shows up to answer these questions? What happens when the cheerleaders in your life get tired and put their pom-poms down? What happens when no one shows up to give you life? I desperately needed the answers to these important life questions. I wanted someone to show up and give me purpose, so I became a pro at looking to others.

I felt like Shirley A. Mason, the woman portrayed in the book *Sybil*. There were two stories told—one that she was a psychiatric patient who suffered from multiple personality disorder and the other that she made up the different personalities to get the attention of her doctor. I'm not sure which story is true, but let's say that she indeed made up the different personalities. What if she started off pretending to be someone she wasn't for affirmation, attention, and love, but along the way lost touch with reality?

This was my story. I longed to be accepted and loved, so I became whomever I needed to be for someone to accept or love me. You may be laughing right now, thinking this woman is really crazy, but how many times have you done something or didn't do something because of your need for someone's affection and affirmation? As women, we're more prone to changing ourselves than men are.

I remember acting like a housewife and preparing a full Thanksgiving meal for my boyfriend at the age of twenty-one. Setting the table, basting a huge turkey, baking homemade macaroni and cheese in the oven, and making stuffing because I hadn't learned how to make my grandmother's dressing and never did. Crazy, but I thought it was what I needed to do in order to keep a man.

I like cooking good, sometimes-healthy twenty-minute meals. But I was giving to my boyfriend what would one day be for my husband. I was single. I should have been traveling, seeing the world, enjoying my college experiences, meeting new people, creating new memories, and having fun, not cooking a full-course Thanksgiving dinner and setting the table like I was a black Martha Stewart at twenty-one years of age. (The devil is a liar!) I tried everything I could to keep him seeing me as someone special. And I did this not only with men, but with everyone. The saddest part to this truth is that I was trying to convince them to see something that I did not even believe.

When I first moved to California, I met two young ladies who strongly suggested, after knowing me for only two weeks, that my style of clothing was outdated. So of course, if they thought I looked outdated and ugly, I needed to dress differently. I allowed them to take me shopping at an outlet, Durant Square, in Oakland, and spent money that I didn't have to buy clothes that I really didn't care for. Yet their perception of me was that I looked so much better, and I believed them. It's crazy how a lie can become your truth.

Years later, I found a picture of myself in one of the outfits they convinced me to purchase and I cracked up laughing. I couldn't believe, at nineteen, that I'd allowed someone dress me like a thirty-six-year-old businesswoman, and not a good one, I might add. I looked horrible.

These small compromises have a long-term impact on decisions we make for ourselves based on someone else's or our own false perception. We start to mistrust or even don't recognize our own voice. It was these little termites that ate away at the foundation of my self-confidence. Some people like us when we're the person they need us to be, but come to despise us once we become the person we were created to be. They're irritated because we have the audacity to be ourselves—to be something different from what they perceived us to be. This may seem minor, but it can snowball into a never-ending marathon.

How draining! I felt old trying to keep up with everyone's perception of what I was supposed to be doing. How I was supposed to raise my kids. What my marriage should look like. How I should dress. What the call on my life should be. What I should do with my money. Who I should be around. I'm not saying to not listen to wisdom—it's more priceless than rubies and is needed in the Land of I am—but people's opinions and perceptions, especially when false, are weeds that have the potential to choke out the truth of who you were created to be.

When my youngest daughter was in second grade, she came to me with a beautiful picture that she creatively colored. She was so excited until I opened my big mouth without even blinking and apparently not even thinking. I said, "Oh, sweetie, it's nice, but you need to color within the lines next time." The look on my baby girl's face was heartbreaking. I had crushed her vision of herself—of being a young and brilliant Picasso—with my opinion.

I did to my daughter what many of us have experienced at some point in our lives; we had someone crush our view of ourselves. I did not realize the conflict I was creating inside her: she was excited and proud of her drawing, yet I was telling her it was not good enough. As the years went on, I saw this conflict within her grow, until she was in the fifth grade, and God opened my eyes to see, embrace, and fight for my daughter's uniqueness.

By the time my daughter was in the fifth grade, the light that used to be in her beautiful brown eyes—the one that told the world she was unapologetically different and loving it—was gone. She started becoming more and more unsure of herself. We signed her up with a new basketball league, and we would see tears forming in her eyes during practice before the game began because she was so afraid of getting the ball and not knowing what to do with it. This was the same girl who did gymnastics for three years and was not afraid to flip off a balancing beam at six years old.

We did not know what was going on with her, but we knew it was more than just being afraid on the basketball court. She started having trouble in school, her grades were dropping, and she was miserable. At first, I thought it was because she had started a new school a year before, not by choice but because we moved and she had to attend school in our district, but as time went on we saw no signs of improvement.

She would be up past nine o'clock, overwhelmed, trying to complete her homework. We would go to her classroom, and her desk would be packed with papers and trash. One time, we asked if the teacher had a garbage bag and filled it up to the top with all the contents in her desk. There were tests, homework assignments that she had completed but never turned in, and incomplete classwork. When we addressed her, she showed confusion as well as frustration at her own behavior.

Fortunately for her, I was a different person, a much better parent, and I had learned that our perception of someone, especially if it's false, can lead to inaccurate assumptions. I realized that my husband and I were getting upset and dealing with the condition, not the cause. We had assumed she wasn't doing well in school because she wasn't trying, until I was reminded of a story told by my middle daughter's fifth-grade teacher five years earlier.

He had stated that the reason why he became a fifth-grade teacher was because he failed the fifth grade two times. He felt stupid and never wanted to go to school again, but then his mother's friend told her about a private school that taught subjects using very creative methods. His fifth-grade math teacher taught him how to do math by using a recorder, and he realized that he understood math and in fact loved it. It turned out that, as an artistic learner, he learned differently from most kids. He not only passed the fifth grade but graduated at the top of his class and went on to college to become a teacher to help other kids like him.

One of my spiritual moms, Dr. Barbara Williams, used to say that if people don't learn the way you teach, then you need to teach the way they learn. That's not always easy with all the politics and red tape that teachers have to go through. When you have forty very different kids and no assistant, it may seem almost impossible to help one or two students who learn differently from the average student.

All of this came back to me one day while my husband and I were lecturing my daughter about her grades. I realized that throughout the years, we were unintentionally and unconsciously telling her she was not smart enough, she was not giving her all, and she was not going to succeed in life if she kept it up. We had been punishing her for learning differently without even realizing it.

So this time I decided to fight for her! I asked the school to test my daughter, which they did. The first time, they brought in a school psychologist to talk to us and that didn't go well, because in all of five minutes, he was trying to label her with ADHD (attention deficit/hyperactivity disorder)—without even talking to her.

I politely shut him down and told him we weren't going to subject her to that type of testing. He was taken off her case and we were assigned a different school psychologist, whom we loved. What we found out amazed us: our daughter's scores revealed that she was on a sixth-grade level. So how was she failing fifth grade?

We also found out that she is a kinesthetic (hands-on) learner, which explained why she took everything apart and rebuilt it the way she thought it should be in her mind and why she would always play with some object in her hands while the teacher was teaching. They assumed she was distracted, when, in reality, having something in her hand helped her focus. The psychologist then told us that my daughter wasn't finishing her classwork because she didn't learn well in an overstimulated atmosphere, so she would be a perfect homeschool candidate.

My husband and I decided to sacrifice our time and the things we had going on to homeschool our daughter. We enrolled her in Hickman Charter School, which puts an emphasis on helping homeschoolers, we also had a friend who was a substitute teacher partner with us to teach some of the courses that we couldn't. It was the best decision of our lives. My daughter's light began to slowly shine once again. The school offered a lot of hands-on learning projects that they hosted in what they called the "Maker's Garage," such as woodworking and even building a robot. Her light was not only shining, but she was confident and happy.

After a full year of homeschool, we put her in a private school that had about twenty-five students in the entire school. They did a lot of hands-on projects and learned at their own pace, and the principal didn't believe in giving homework. My daughter excelled. She now wants to be an engineer, and I'm so curious to see what this young woman creates.

Her bedroom is like the workshop of a mad scientist. I'm used to going into her room and confiscating things that might harm her when she is not home, but what I no longer do is stop her mind from creating new ideas. I don't stop her from coloring outside the lines; as a matter of fact, I encourage it.

Now what would have happened if I'd made her stay within the lines? What would have happened if we would have labeled her a bad student or a failure? What would have happened if we allowed the school psychologist to label her with a condition she didn't have? I'll tell you what would have happened: my daughter probably would have believed our inaccurate assumptions about her because we were her parents and she trusted us. She would have believed she was different in a negative way. She would have continued to be frustrated, and maybe even depressed, because everyone was telling her that how she learns is wrong, which to a child would mean that something is wrong with her.

Her dreams of being an engineer could have, perhaps, been crushed. How could she accomplish such a thing when she was flunking out of fifth grade and made to feel stupid, and had no support from the two people who were supposed to be her greatest cheerleaders? She would be one who was misunderstood—a tragedy, another statistic, like so many other kids whose parents don't have the knowledge that we were blessed to obtain. My daughter, like many other children, is not a problem kid. Her misunderstood behavior was her way of making a conscious decision to rebel against being anything other than herself. She was ripping the labels off.

I have some questions for you: What labels have been placed on you? Do you find yourself afraid to be anything outside what others already believe about you? My heart breaks because of how many children right now are living up to a label that was placed on them at a young age. If you were labeled as a child, as I was, you start to truly believe everyone else can read that label or those labels; you believe it's noticeable and unacceptable.

Remember Superman? Nothing could kill him but Kryptonite. I want to tell you that assumptions are just as powerful as the Kryptonite that hung around Superman's neck; it literally suppresses the power within you. Kryptonite (labels/assumptions) keeps you from soaring in your purpose. As powerful as Superman was, Kryptonite was the one thing that Lex Luthor could use to stop him from being the super-hero that the world loved and needed. Superman needed help to remove the thing that had the power to defeat him, and you too might need a little help to remove whatever is preventing you from being who you were created to be.

Who told us that drawing outside the lines was wrong, inappropriate, or ugly? Who told us that we should box in our creativity, play it safe, and stay within the lines? By the way, who came up with the term *constructive criticism*? The root word is *critic*, and a critic is one who expresses an unfavorable opinion of something or one who judges the merits of literary, artistic, or musical works, especially one who does so professionally. I understand the concept of constructive criticism, but there are times when it's misappropriated.

At times, it's been used to keep people from coloring outside the lines; it destroys the imagination of the child within. I didn't realize that my constructive criticism was simply criticism in my daughter's eyes—that it had no real merit: "Oh, that's nice, but you need to color within the lines next time. It will be more beautiful." What is more beautiful than allowing your imagination to create the life you dream of?

Now don't get me wrong. We all need wisdom, guidance, encouragement, and yes, sometimes correction. But if you find yourself tearing someone down with negative opinions and inaccurate assumptions and calling it "constructive criticism," it's an oxymoron! We say, "Be different," but the moment someone colors outside the lines, we want to correct it. It makes us feel uncomfortable because we've been taught to fear different instead of embracing it. We've become a people prone to automatically look to others for approval, and when we don't get it, we find ourselves questioning our value. In the same manner, we're also prone to immediately judge things before we take the time to understand them.

We've played it safe far too long, and it's time to rebel. To rebel means to resist any authority, control, or tradition.

This definition doesn't encourage us to rebel against people, but against tradition, against the control of other people's opinions when they have no real merit, and against what the world says is normal or beautiful.

It's time to define what extraordinary looks like, and it looks like you being you. It's time to do and create something unforgettable and unimaginable.

## Reflection in the Mirror

They say I'm beautiful and intelligent as can be;
Why can't I see this reflection that they say is me?

They say I'm strong and powerful,
with a call on my life;
Why can't I see this reflection that they say is me?

They say if I lead, others will follow,
that my character will draw them all;
Why can't I see this reflection that they say is me?

They say I am humble and that my heart
is full of love and affection;
Why can't I see this reflection they say is me?

They say I'm more precious than silver and gold,
but people always tease me and treat me so cold;
Why can't I see this reflection they say is me?

HE says I'm going to be successful
and prosperous one day,
but that's not what my teachers used to say;
Why don't they see this reflection HE says is me?

They say my smile lights up a room,
but do they know my heart is filled
with sadness and gloom?
Why can't I see this reflection they say is me?

I stared in the mirror, wondering where it could be;
Where is this reflection that I cannot see?

Then suddenly HE told me to close my eyes,
and what amazing vision I saw arise!
It was my reflection, to my surprise—
it was always there waiting for me
to believe on the inside.

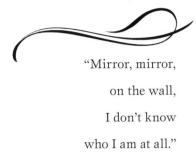

"Mirror, mirror,

on the wall,

I don't know

who I am at all."

—*Tiffany James*

CHAPTER SEVEN

# Mirror, Mirror

C an I ask you two serious questions: Do you really know who you are? Did you know that it takes faith to believe in who you are?

Faith is believing in something you can't see. There is nothing outside yourself that can define who you really are; you can't trust and depend on what you see or don't see in the natural. You must trust that inner voice and those hidden jewels that give you clues as to how amazing you truly are. In the words of poet Audre Lorde, "If I didn't define myself for myself, I would be crunched into other people's fantasies for me and eaten alive."[12]

A mirror is any reflecting surface that gives a faithful representation, image, or idea of something else. Are there people or things you're using as a mirror to reflect who you really are? Are you finding yourself always turning to those things or people to affirm you because you really don't know your worth? If you don't know who you are, the world is eager to tell you.

For instance, take the story of Evil Queen in *Snow White and the Seven Dwarfs*. If you remember the original story by the Brothers Grimm, Snow White's real mother was a kind and lovely woman who was truly adored by all the people in her land. She carried just one sadness—she wanted a child but was childless.

One winter day, she was sewing while gazing at the falling snow outside her window. A bird flew by, startling the queen, and she pricked her finger. The story states that a single drop of blood fell on the snow, and as the queen looked at the blood-stained snow, she wished for a daughter with skin as white as snow, lips as red as blood, and hair as black as ebony.

Soon after that, the queen got her wish and named her daughter Snow White. Sadly, the queen died shortly afterward, and Snow White's father remarried a new queen, who we have come to know as the Evil Queen.

Evil Queen dabbled in black magic and had a mirror that she often consulted. It reminded her that she was the fairest in all the land, more beautiful than any other. Then one day, all that changed. See, the mirror could speak nothing but truth, and now there was another more beautiful than her—Snow White. Immediately, Evil Queen viewed herself differently.

You might wonder what this story has to do with you or this book, and I say *everything*. Many of us have the same mirror complex; for so long, we have looked to and depended on something else to tell us who we are, each time believing the mirror reflects the absolute truth of that. We've been psychologically trained to look outward instead of inward. What a tragedy, that we look to someone or something that did not create us to define us.

Evil Queen was told over and over again that she was beautiful, but she didn't believe it within. She continued to look to the magic mirror to tell her who she was and desired to be. The moment she compared herself was the moment she felt and eventually became less-than. The moment we compare ourselves is the moment we too become less, because we are perceiving that someone or something is prettier, uglier, better, worse, taller, bigger, or more successful than we are.

That's just like a rose (work with me if you will) being intimidated by a lily or vice versa. You can't compare them because both are beautiful flowers with their own unique characteristics; both are preferred, and both are exquisite. I know it might sound a little silly, but that's what we do all the time, especially women. We constantly compare ourselves to someone who was created differently, inside and out, on purpose for a purpose. It's asinine!

You cannot continue to look to people and things, making them your mirror, because that equation will never add up. So many people are dependent on someone or something to show up and give them value. What if these things fail to reflect the real you? What if they tell you something you don't want to hear? What if their perception of you is inaccurate? Where does that you leave you?

To give some sense of identity, let's answer some questions: What if that new, expensive car you purchased and bragged to everyone about gets repossessed? What if your husband turns out to not be your Prince Charming after all? What if your wife is not the queen you thought she was? What if you lose that amazing job? What if you can no longer afford the big five-bedroom, three-bathroom house you posted on social media? What if the kid you sacrificed everything for decides to act a fool and make decisions that could be detrimental to his or her future while embarrassing you in the same breath? What if the body you had when you were in your twenties is nothing more than a long-lost memory? What if the close friends you thought had your back were just that—a thought? What if the dreams you had as a child seem so impossible because you made some bad decisions that altered the course of your life, and it's been hard to get back on track? What if you're still dealing with the broken pieces of your childhood, and they keep haunting and reminding you that you are broken?

You cannot continue to look outside yourself to find yourself.

Now I know that the things I mentioned above all play major roles in our lives, but they do not define us. It's time to get a hammer and crack the mirrors you've depended on for so long, into irrevocable pieces. Or maybe the mirror has already been shattered by one or more of the things I mentioned. Either way, those things never reflected the real you, so stop picking up the broken glass of perception.

Remember, a mirror is something regarded as accurately and faithfully representing something else. You need to identify what you're looking to. Does it accurately represent you? Your reflection might faithfully show up, but what is it showing you about yourself daily? A mirror is also any reflective surface set in a frame or attached to a handle used for viewing oneself.

It's time to turn away or let go of the handle! Stop viewing yourself through distorted lenses. My spiritual father, Brent Lokker, says, "Stop deluding yourself by unsound reasoning." A mirror only depicts what's on the surface. It is time to move beyond that and go deep within to find the treasures hidden on the inside of you.

My heart aches because we have given such things as Facebook, reality shows, commercials, movies, videos, people's opinions, our careers, and songs the authority to say what we should look, sound, feel, and act like. I know people who have potential to do great things, but they never try to step out to follow their dreams. They compare themselves out of doing it. Yes, that's right. They *compare* themselves out of opportunities to do something amazing and maybe a little different.

For a long time, I was just too afraid to pull the curtain. I was afraid to come forth being my true authentic self, instead continuing to look to things to reflect my worth. Yet little by little my mirrors were cracking, and I was being forced to step out on stage while trying to make sense of the shattered pieces of my life all around me.

My spiritual mom, Dr. Barbara Williams, used to tell me all the time, "What God has placed in you is for me, and I want it." It's not always about us. We can't continue to be selfish and self-centered. The world is waiting for you to release what God has placed in you for them. I want to encourage you to gain the confidence, as well as the courage, to pull the rope and stop hiding behind the curtain. The world is waiting on you to take a bow.

## Simple Cares of Life

Looking at things we can't comprehend,
looking at situations and people
from outside, not within ...

Finding ourselves thinking, *Life isn't fair;*
*it's full of cruelty and wasteful thinking.*
And you ask the question, "Is God there?"

Not knowing there is no new thing under the sun,
or what you prayed for God has already done.

So don't be dismayed about Simple Cares of Life;
you might not understand,
but find strength and encouragement
in God—not man.

"Being exposed can

bring the freedom

you've been longing."

—*Tiffany James*

# CHAPTER EIGHT

# Pulling Back the Curtain

P ulling the curtain back is not always easy. The rope is thick, heavy, tangled, and stubborn. In 2006, my family and I relocated to a small town, Oakdale, California. I didn't realize it at the time, but God was about to pull back the curtain of my life. I had no time to prepare.

At the time, I had been recruited, from my job of almost eight years at North American Title, to Alliance Title Company, and had been working there for a year. The new position challenged me in so many ways, but I accepted and conquered.

When I first got hired eight years earlier, it was a refinance market. Like every job I ever had, I quickly moved up the corporate ladder. I'm a natural-born leader, and I led and managed without thinking about it. My clients loved me because I love people and every client felt like they were my only client. It seemed like every escrow I opened, I successfully closed.

Confidence in the workplace was never a problem for me, but when I started at Alliance Title Company, they required all their escrow officers, especially those who wanted to move up financially, to do both refinance and purchase transactions. I was a skilled escrow officer when it came to refinances, but for years I stayed away from purchases in the escrow industry because of having to deal with the buyer, seller, their individual agents, and the ton of documents, not to mention the financial calculations of it all.

In the beginning, fear and intimidation gripped me because I was looking at and comparing myself to the other escrow officers in the office. I felt inadequate and insignificant, and thought that they must be wondering how in the world I'd made it this long in the industry without learning how to do a purchase.

I questioned my decision to leave my old company where I had security, but the reality was there was no turning back. The only reason I questioned it was because my old job made me feel important and successful, and this new company was jeopardizing that image of myself. The office I was placed in, with my two assistants, had two other escrow officers, both of whom had been in the business for a long time. They knew the business well, but because of a few unfortunate events, both were let go from the company. I moved up to the position of branch manager by default.

I now had my own beautiful office in the Brookside area of Stockton, California. I had three beautiful girls and an amazing husband (although at the time I didn't recognize it) at home, and was making over $100,000 a year. I had just purchased my second home, had two cars that were paid off, and was traveling. There was nothing that my family or I wanted for, but I still felt empty. Dry and barren. With all my so-called success, nothing quenched this longing in me.

One morning, before my assistants arrived, I stared out my office window, crying and praying. That's when I heard these words: "No eyes have seen, no ear has heard, and no mind can conceive all that I have in store for you." The words soothed my parched soul, giving me an oasis of hope. But as time went by without any doors of opportunity opening for me, I questioned if it was merely a mirage of hope. Did my heart's desire for more than just a nine-to-five job create an illusion for me?

Just like the body needs water, the soul needs hope. I was no longer satisfied and felt like I was dying—like the walls were closing in on me. One day as I sat at my desk staring at the walls, a question popped into my head: "What if the walls could talk?" This is what I wrote:

## If the Walls Could Talk

IT WAS ALMOST TIME to go home, as I watched the digital clock on the computer change from 4:59 to 5:00. I finished up my last folder, waiting for the ink to dry after using a fine-point black Sharpie to write a new escrow number and client's name. I don't know why, but I was tired of writing on the same manila folders, in the same exact way, and then filing them in the same black file cabinet as I did for the last I don't know how many years. I sat there wondering what was different this day.

Then I realized it was me. The passion for the career I thought I wanted and needed was lost. As I sat there staring at the walls, wondering what I was doing there, the four walls began shouting at me, "How long will you sit here? How long do we have to watch you die daily?" They continued, "You are becoming just like us—still, plain, and cornered."

My eyes flooded with tears as I stared into the emptiness in front of me. I could feel the coldness of the walls behind me, whispering in the air, "Why doesn't she just get up? Why won't she move? She is so scared. I wish we could push her." I could hear the walls' words circling in the air as their truth taunted me, "Why does she turn on the light when she arrives each morning, when she lives in darkness? She is withering away from lack of hope, enclosed in a box while calling it an office. When is she going to realize that her destiny is not within these four walls? If only we could just push her out so we could stop looking at our own reflection."

The right wall said to the left, "I get so angry because the people we shelter have the ability, unlike us, to move and they don't. They stay stuck, as if they were created to be a wall, created to corner in the giftings they possess. Always saying, 'If I just ... If I just had the opportunity.' I hate to hear them say this same thing while sitting in the same chair, in the same position, with the same thoughts, doing the same thing. Why can't they create an opportunity? The word if must stand for 'individual failure.' Do they realize they create their own blockage?"

Suddenly, they stopped and sighed their last bit of disappointment of me. I went to turn off the lights as one more comment was uttered from the side wall that held the light switch, "We will be stuck yet another night in darkness, but she will be living in darkness for the rest of her life if she does not move."

That hit me as I stood in the doorway of my office, frazzled by the very conversation of the walls. Walls that shielded my insecurities Monday through Friday. I wondered how they knew my innermost fears. At that moment, I realized the walls were closing in on me and I could hear the beams snapping.

I realized that when you are entangled with destiny but refuse to move, sometimes the walls of frustration will close in on you, forcing you to move.

I must say the walls did speak. They spoke loud and clear when my boss came in and stated that the company was laying off another group of escrow officers—and I was in that group. I had a contract, so I wasn't so worried about them laying me off; as a matter of fact, I started putting a strategy together. With the money I would get from my contract, I planned to open a small greeting card store to display my writings.

Little did I know; the company was going to file for bankruptcy and would not have to honor my contract. Two homes, two car insurances, three kids, a husband finishing up paramedic school, credit card bills, and no job! Then to top it off, I had no desire to go back to a nine-to-five job that I was sure would result in me dying a slow death. Now the only thing I had to do was tell my wonderful husband, who must see everything for it to make sense, that I felt like I wasn't supposed to go back to work and that somehow, we would be able to take care of all our expenses.

At first, he looked at me as if I'd truly lost my mind and needed to find it, but after putting everything on the table and examining it, we both came to a cool compromise: after my unemployment ran out, I would seek part-time work that would be close to home and something fulfilling for me.

I mentioned my need for a fulfilling part-time job to our group at Bible study to see if anyone knew of any open positions. A friend told me that she knew someone who worked at Family Support Network, and it sounded like the perfect job. I love encouraging and helping people—it's such a natural gift for me—and I thought about how many women I could encourage at the center.

It turned out this friend of a friend was no longer employed there but with a company called Homestead Senior Care. It was a job and I would still be helping people, so I applied and was hired as a sales rep. I really enjoyed working there but still wasn't fulfilled. After I was there for two months, my manager told me that the company was about to contract with Bristol, a hospice clinic, and that I would be the sales rep for both.

My first hospice client was a beautiful woman in her early fifties—a brilliant teacher and an adventurous woman who was slowly withering away of cancer. Her beloved husband wanted to honor her wish to spend her last days at home. As I walked into their home and took one look at the frail woman whose bones could be seen through her thin, pale skin, I had to head straight to the bathroom so they wouldn't see me crying.

I gathered myself because I needed to be professional and had a job to do, then walked back to the living room where she would be spending her last days. Pictures on the wall detailed the life of this once-vibrant woman. The hospice nurse was gently getting her comfortable, while I was supposed to sit down with the husband to sign all the paperwork and collect a check. Hospice would be out four times a week, and our company would be there the other three days, but insurance did not cover our services.

The husband couldn't stop telling me about his wife and her many accomplishments. He was so distraught, that I couldn't bring myself to ask him for the check, so instead I went to Starbucks and bought us coffee. When I got back, I allowed him to talk more about his wife. Finally, I collected the courage to ask him for the check and to sign papers. That's when my biggest fear smacked me dead in my face.

He was irritated with me, and rightfully so. I apologized, told him to call me when he was ready, and left. When I returned to the office, my manager was not so understanding. I didn't care though; I told her the company needed to rethink its procedures because asking someone for a check and to sign papers the day their loved one is being brought home to die is unethical in my book. I did go back the next day because I also understood business.

I worked for the company a full year, and my time there was so much fun because it's not about what you do, but who you are. I made the position work for me instead of me working to fit the position. I did get the same results but went about it with a different approach than what was expected. I visited senior centers, going to their line dancing events and bringing little treats for their gatherings. Instead of trying to sell them something, I got involved in their world. They learned what we offered, and when they needed the services, they knew who they could trust. I also attended the funeral of one of my clients because I had become very close with her daughter. It was about relationship, not about business.

Then came another shift within the company, and I no longer had the passion for the work. I still felt like something was missing. My husband and I discussed it, and he faithfully reminded me about our two homes, three kids, two car insurances, utilities, food, credit card bills, and tuition, as if I had a case of temporary amnesia. I wanted to honor him and knew it was more difficult for a man to not think about all the things he needs to take care of because a real man is a provider. So I did what I always do, and that was pray. I really felt like my time at this job was ending, which had me a little anxious, but I also felt like God was calling something within me to come forth.

The next morning, I got dressed for work, dropped my girls off at school, and headed for work. While I was driving, my husband called and said that he had been praying and came up with a plan. Finances would be tight, but we could survive. I was so grateful but could still feel the uncertainty in his voice, so I told him to let me talk to my manager to see if I could just cut back on my hours.

My manager was in the conference room when I arrived, and she waved me in to join her. I entered, wondering what was going on and hoping she wasn't going to add more work to my plate. She explained that the company was downsizing, and they had to let go of one sales rep. Now there were only two sales reps, me and an older gentleman in his late-sixties or early seventies. He was the one they were going to let go that day. I told her that before she made her decision, I needed to tell her my dilemma of desiring less hours.

She looked at me and said, "Let me lay you off, then, because you probably would get more money through unemployment than working less than thirty hours a week." That way she could keep the other sales representative who had been with them a long time, since it would be hard for him to start over at his age.

I was laid off that day, and I knew what I was sensing from God concerning my life was about to take off. Well, at least I thought so. See, by this time, even though I was about to stop working and would have unemployment coming in, I had also just co-authored and released my first book, my husband was still working and believing that within that year he would become a fireman, I was being booked and paid to speak at many different venues, my three girls seemed like they were transitioning well with all the changes in our home, and now I had the freedom to follow my dreams.

But when the curtain is forced open, things don't always look so pretty. It's like being caught with your pants down and your eyes bucked. You're standing on stage and everyone is staring, trying to figure out what in the world is going on because it looked like you had it all together. Shortly after my brief moment of happiness, my world was flipped upside down. I was left with nothing but chaos and didn't know how to sort through it all. You've already had front-row seats thus far, so let me share what my stage looked like then.

From 2002 till 2006, most people from the outside looking in would have envied my life. By 2007, they would have pitied it. The best job I ever had ended in 2006. We eventually had to short sale our first home, and our second home was foreclosed on while we were trying everything in our power to either keep it or sell it. We used up all our savings and my 401k in the process. Every door closed regarding me traveling to speak. We struggled in our finances, not even making it from one paycheck to another. My oldest daughter was wrestling with her identity because we had moved to a small, predominantly white community during her crucial teen years. No more eating at the fancy restaurants we loved, no more trips, no more shopping, and no money to keep us busy.

As a result, my husband and I had to face a truth. We weren't happy. I felt rejected by him, and at the same time I was dealing with feeling like a failure as a mom. I felt overlooked, misunderstood, and unloved. I was on stage, eyes bucked, and pants down, and completely exposed! I was embarrassed, frustrated, and disappointed, and I felt like a failure. I literally felt like Carrie in the movie that shares her name. Voices echoed in my head: "They're all going to laugh at you. They're all going to laugh at you." Those voices were so clear and strong even though they had no real validity.

But what we call a tragedy in life can be God's grace at work. I define *grace* as the ability to do that which you can't do in and of yourself. It's a supernatural strength.

The curtain was pulled back, and I was forced to address everything that came to the forefront. At the same time, I had just started visiting a church in my community. A lady who worked at my daughter's preschool had invited me to church to hear her sing, and I'd promised her I would come. At hearing her, I wanted to burst out laughing, because even though she had the voice of an angel, she was singing country gospel.

I am a down-to-earth, soulful African-American girl from the South Side of Chicago. I couldn't find a rhythm to clap my hands or do my Southern church dance to the country gospel lyrics. I knew it was God calling me to go to the church because there was no way I would voluntarily choose to attend a church where they sang country gospel every Sunday.

The name of the church was called Oak Valley, and I'm so glad that God directed my steps. I don't believe in coincidence. The people in this church carried such an authentic love for people. To my surprise, the next Sunday there was a different worship team. Even though it was still a different style of worship than I was used to, the music was beautiful, and it wasn't country gospel. (The beautiful woman who invited me loved country gospel, and she only sang every so often because the pastor allowed a place for her gifting for that type of worship.)

Coming to that church literally changed my life. I never felt out of place even though the members were predominantly Caucasian with a few Hispanic families. On that day I realized that this was going to be my church home, I walked into the 11:00 a.m. service and the worship pastor was leading a song called "The Stand," written by Michael W. Smith. The words gripped my heart and I surrendered everything to God.

At the time, my life looked like a thousand-piece puzzle and I had no clue how to put it together. I chose to surrender to the One who did. His grace was the strength that I needed.

Okay, you know it's an inspirational aha moment. You ready?

### Life

Every day of your life becomes a struggle
when there is no direction.
Emptiness destroying the soul within;
Asking, "Why face your tomorrows when
still battling your yesterdays?"
Praying and standing on what FAITH you have left;
Hoping that every obstacle faced might somehow
show restitution for things you couldn't escape.
Entangled with purpose and opposition.

Feelings of curiosity—pieces of a
puzzle—something is missing.
Yet beauty and mystery lie beneath.


Believing in the miracle that something wonderful
might happen with the life given—never chosen.
Believing in the old saying "It's never
too late" may very well be true;
now demanding into the heavens—
"Release what is due!"


Then, in the midst of confusion, you can
look at something as simple and innocent as
a smile on the face of a newborn child—
see the awesomeness of life.
The simple reminder of the child that lies within ...
Pure, untouched, as if you were
completely without sin.


Appreciating HE chose such a simple thing to draw you near
so, HE could whisper words of comfort
and confirmation in your ear.
Saying, "I will never leave you nor forsake you,
and My purpose will speak in due season;
And everything you went through, my
child—YES, it was for a reason.

> So don't you fret, and don't you dare worry for all
> you went through, and even what you are going through
> right now is and will forever be for God's glory!
> It's just simply life."

Yes, during confusion, God took my chaotic life and made it beautiful. Sometimes you don't even know that something is missing until you receive it. The curtain had been pulled back. I realized that all my accomplishments masked the awful truth that I felt incomplete, worthless, unloved, and lost.

One day I was sitting in Starbucks trying to write, because writing has always been a safe place for me. The blank pages carried my secrets and gave me some sense of peace. A woman in her late-fifties approached me. She had the most beautiful, vibrant, and contagious spirit. She said, "I just wanted you to know that you have a smile that is so beautiful." She then said something else about my smile, though I don't remember what.

I thanked her, and we chatted briefly, and I gave her a copy of the book that I'd co-authored with a few other powerful women. Since then I've never looked at my smile quite the same; I realized that I could make somebody's day with something as simple as my smile.

What I didn't know that day was this same woman would play a crucial role in my life. About a year after that encounter, I was walking on a trail in my community while encouraging someone over the phone. I heard a voice fly by, saying, "Preach it, sista!" I turned around and realized that it was the same woman from Starbucks. More time passed. Then I was standing outside my church greeting people with the youth when she walked up and introduced herself as Bernie. We greeted one another with a hug, I was able to connect her face with the previous encounters, and the rest has been history.

This woman was a tool in God's hand. He used her to bring healing to my life. She has a true gift for inner healing, which was exactly what I needed. She always saw beneath the surface and went straight to the source of my pain on a deep level. We all need that person who can see what we can't, while carefully restoring our sight. I realized that among the other things I mentioned earlier, the root of what I was dealing with was rejection and unforgiveness. I saw how I stuffed my pain and kept moving on with life. But all that junk was lying dormant, waiting for the opportune time to shows its ugly face.

I also realized that my husband and I were running a scam because our marriage was not what everyone, including ourselves, perceived it to be. My husband is a quiet and sometimes passive man. My hidden issues caused me to perceive everything he did or said as rejection. I felt like I wasn't interesting or attractive enough for him to want to spend time with me and thought he didn't care enough about me to deal with the things that were bothering me.

The reality was he didn't understand what was bothering me. He wasn't equipped to fix my brokenness, nor did he sign up to do so. In saying that, he did have things he needed to work on regarding communication. Even though it affected me, I later realized this wasn't about me. He didn't know how to communicate and express his emotions, but he was trying his best. He loved me the only way he knew how, but not the way my unrealistic expectations demanded. I was making him pay for every person who had ever hurt or rejected me, and this caused me to make stupid decisions that almost cost me my marriage.

I'm so glad God's grace is sufficient. I'm so glad that my husband and I made Him the glue of our marriage and that He held us together during a fragile time. God knew we needed help because neither one of us had the tools to deal with our problems in a healthy way.

Therefore, He sent Dr. Barbara, who later became my spiritual mom, to counsel us during a time when our marriage was in jeopardy. She helped us recognize that our issues were not so much marital, but individual issues we brought into the marriage. These issues were hindering us from growing and having a beautifully healthy marriage. She taught us what marriage was in God's eyes and not our false expectations of what it should be. This amazing woman truly has a God-given gift to heal marriages and I'm grateful that we were recipients of that gift.

Through my journey of healing with both Bernie and Dr. Barbara walking right beside me in different areas and ways, I saw so many things about my life that I never had seen before. These things were foundational truths that I needed in order to heal.

When your eyes are opened, you must seek the truth with every ounce of curiosity in your very being. Too often we seek to hold on to our illusions of the truth. Illusions are a distortion of our senses, and they distort the truth! Your spirit cannot see the blessings when the eyes of your soul keep seeing the insignificant things of this world.

It's time for the eyes of your soul to be opened.

## See Me

I AM NOT A product of passion, but the substance of purpose.

I am not just the pain of birth, yet the joy and reason for life.

I am not the burden of your back, I am the blessing to your future.

I am not your mistake, yet your gift.

I am not your headache, but your hope.

Remember, I am a part of you—not necessarily a reflection of you.

Do you understand that my existence was predestined?

The only thing I know—I am part of God's perfect plan.

Do you know who I am now?

Do you see me for who I am?

I am your child.

CHAPTER NINE

# I Now See

Optical illusions are common because our vision often dominate our other senses. For instance, if you walked into a room and a group of people began to whisper, you'd think that they were talking about you, when, they were already whispering about something that occurred right before you entered. You see how easy it is to grab hold of something that isn't the truth and base your actions on a mere illusion as you walk away feeling rejected?

When I began my journey of healing, God started removing my optical illusions and taught me how to see things through His eyes. I'm here to tell you what I saw was beauty hidden under ashes.

When you decide to trust the Father's eyes, you'll see that He makes everything beautiful in His time. When the curtain of my life was pulled back, I saw everything more clearly, especially with my eldest daughter. I saw a familiar pattern in how I dealt with her; it was the same way my mom had dealt with me when she didn't understand my behavior, except I dished it out through religion.

I was trying so hard to not be like my mom—to make sure my daughter didn't make the same mistakes I made—that I ended up causing her to experience the same rejection as I did. She ended up feeling like she could never measure up, as I was trying to make her be perfect so I could feel like a good mom—a better mom than my mother—and I failed terribly.

I say this all the time: what's in you will inevitably come out of you. I found myself lashing out at my daughter in such a harsh way, and each time I felt horrible because it was not my intention (I later learned that it was not my mom's either). I had to recognize that I had the spirit of control. They say where there is control, there is fear. I feared my daughter making the same mistakes as I did, just as my mom feared me making the same mistakes as she did. So I tried to control her life, and when it didn't fit my expectations, I called her out on it. I created struggles for my daughter that only God could undo.

Many parents don't realize that some of their children's issues are the result of their issues. Children aren't even allowed to be kids. Their childhood experiences are full of anger, dysfunction, inadequacy, brokenness, molestation, fear, demoralization, and whatever else goes on within the four walls called home. I had to realize I was given an amazing responsibility to steward three incredible human beings; I was chosen as a vessel to bring forth God's destiny.

If we as parents can really see our children as His, that might change the way we handle or mishandle our kids. Maybe if we would look to God, the One who created them, we would better understand how to raise them. For all the mothers reading this right now, we were chosen to carry and nurture destiny! For all the fathers, you were chosen to cover, protect, and affirm that destiny! Yes, we were chosen to be keepers of God's precious promise. Love your child for who he or she is; God makes no mistakes.

Maybe even think back to when you were a child and felt misunderstood. Maybe there was a time when you were labeled by your parents' perception of you. If so, did that alter how you viewed yourself? We must remember that we were chosen to be their first teachers, and we were given the authority to lay down the foundation on which they will build.

I must admit that my eldest daughter had a very unstable foundation. I'm so grateful that God had a jackhammer of love that broke up the road I paved for her that would lead her down a path of destruction. I learned and am still learning how to release my girls and give them permission to experience their own journeys, and that I don't have to be fearful that they will repeat my mistakes. I also had to give them room to make their own choices and had to learn to study all three of them to see how unique each one is. Especially with my eldest daughter, I had to learn to let go.

A few years back when she was leaving for college, I was so proud of her but so afraid to let go. I remember having this amazing epiphany that I shared on my blog and want to share with you, called "Letting Go and Making Room":

## Letting Go and Making Room …

I GAZED AT THE frosted-glass picture frame across from where I was sitting in my living room. I was trying to remember the emotions I felt during the specific time the photo was taken. The picture captured my youngest daughter, a day after she was born, in the arms of my oldest daughter, who was eight years old. You would think the puddle of rain that dropped steadily from the bank of my eyes like a leaking faucet was because of the memory of bringing my precious baby girl into this world, but it wasn't. Echoes of silence drew me closer to the picture, and all I could see was my oldest daughter's big beautiful smile and puppy-dog eyes. She was so young, and the innocence in her eyes called out to me, "I will always be your baby girl."

I slid out of my comfortable chair and managed to crawl over to my lampstand to grab for her. Picking up that frame gave me a sense of comfort, as if I was picking her up and holding her tightly in my arms. The photo started to reveal something that had been hidden from me all this time. It began to give me answers to questions concerning my oldest daughter, that I'd had throughout the years as she transitioned from my little girl, to a teenager, and now to a young adult.

See, it had been me and her against the world the first three years of her life. Who else other than God was going to love her unconditionally the way that I did? She was my firstborn and I was her first love. She was mine and I, in return, was hers. I was the first person who held her in my arms, and yes, I was her first kiss. I was the first person to ever hold her hand, dry her tears, and sing her to sleep. In the picture she was holding in her arms another person she would have to share me with. She smiled big for the camera as she held her baby sister the best she could due to her arm being broken at school just a few weeks earlier.

I didn't even recognize it then, but as I found myself staring at the picture, I realized that she was very excited, but just like her arm, she was very fragile as well. My mother's intuition must have not been tuned in to how hard it must have been for her to let me go and share me with not only one but now two sisters. Not to mention that I'd also married two years before that!

I gripped the side edges of the frame even harder, wishing I could go back in time to let her know how much she meant to me—that no one could ever take her place in my heart.

Do you ever wish you could go back in time with the wisdom that you have now? You know, go back to the time before your children no longer desired to hold your hand because they wanted to be a big girl or boy. Before you had to hear the words, "Mom, don't kiss me in front of my friends." You know, before they started picking out their clothes on their own, before they started closing their bedroom door, before they started reading books on their own, and before your singing was the last thing they wanted to hear before going to bed (lol). Or before they wanted to hang out with friends instead of being home having fun with you. Do you ever wish you could go back to the times when they used to tell you everything? To the moments when you were the greatest person in their eyes, who could fix anything and do no wrong?

My beautiful daughter is now eighteen years old, and yesterday I had to loosen my grip a little and let go as we moved her into her college dorm room. Can you say bittersweet? Looking at her picture today, I now know how she must have felt when she had to loosen her grip and learn to share me. My baby girl had to make room in her heart as our family was expanding. I can only imagine how she must have felt when she realized I wasn't perfect and was capable of making huge mistakes. Or how she felt the first time I said something that hurt her even though I didn't mean it. I can better understand how she felt when other things in my life were stressing me out, but I couldn't really talk to her about it, leaving her to wonder if the problem was her. I know how hard it was for her to hear me say, "There are some things that you're going to have to figure out on your own."

Today while gazing into my daughter's eyes, the photo allowed me to grasp a better understanding of some of the emotions she had to work through, because I now find myself experiencing some of those same emotions. I am the one who has to make room in my heart as her world expands. I am the one who is now realizing she is not perfect and that she is capable of making mistakes. I am the one who must learn not to take it personally when she says things she doesn't mean. I am the one learning that there are some things that she'd rather not talk to me about. I am the one who can hear her saying back to me, "Mom, you have to let me figure things out for myself."

God used this precious life to save my life. I started off as the teacher in her life and ended up becoming the student. I am truly grateful for the "before" times. They are my memories captured in my heart, which is where she will always live no matter where she is. I am so proud of her.

I haven't made all the right decisions as a mom, but one right decision I made was training her up in the ways of the Lord. She accepted Jesus as her Lord and Savior. As a mom, that gives me peace because I am assured that He will never leave her or forsake her. He will be with her always, even to the end of the earth. She has started her college journey and she is not alone! Yesterday was not a goodbye but a day when I had to make room in my heart for her to grow—and make room in my heart as her world expands.

With tears of gratitude, I say thank you to God, my husband who is an amazing dad, her sisters, my church family, her grandparents, and the host of aunties, uncles, and friends who have helped me raise her. It truly does take a village to raise a family. So many have helped us in this transition, and all I can say is my God is awesome. This is what it truly means to be wealthy.

To my baby girl I say thank you for allowing me to love you and impart to you. Thank you for helping me become not only a better mom but also a better person. You are truly a super star! P.S. To my mom and dad... I now understand!

---

Yes, I was on stage and forced to deal with my chaotic life. It was the best thing that ever happened to me—a long, amazing journey of healing. God seemingly moved me out to the middle of nowhere (well, the cowboy capital of the world) and hid me so He could heal me. I was stripped of everything I thought I needed to feel complete, whole, and accepted.

He was dealing with my rejection and the spirit of anger that I carried and had learned how to mask. He was shattering the mirror of the false perception that I saw myself through.

He healed my marriage and taught me to love my husband for who he was and not to try to make him who I wanted him to be, so that everyone else can say, "You are one lucky chick." Well, we are learning each other and I can honestly say I *am* one lucky chick.

God taught me how to be a mother through the teachers He placed all around me to teach me how to love my children for who they were, not what I thought they should be. I learned the power of forgiveness, and I learned that when you truly forgive, you release people from the debt of owing you anything in return. I also heard and learned that forgiveness is also giving up the hope that the past could be different. The reality is, time is the one thing we can never get back, so it's not fair to hold someone hostage for a mistake that they can't go back and change.

I believe the most important thing I learned was to love myself. To be true to myself. My mistakes do not define me. It is the courage to acknowledge, address, heal, and learn from those mistakes that will speak long after I leave this world. It's not about what I have or don't have. It's not about how I speak, how I look, what job I have, the car I drive, if I have the perfect family, or if I come from the perfect family. All that matter is that I was created to be me and God doesn't make mistakes. He made me exactly the way I am. He stripped from me everything that I looked to as my mirror and gave me a clear perspective on life. He pulled off all the labels others put on me and I put on myself, removing everything that altered my true identity.

There are so many stories that I could share with you, but they're not for this book. I would be writing forever, and what was meant to be an encouragement would turn into a mystery novel. I believe I moved to Oakdale because God knew I was ready to heal and He knew who He was going to use to reach me. I'm learning more about myself every day, maturing daily. I am free! I'm breathing! Breathing in and out total acceptance. I found my joy, my peace, my courage, my confidence, my boldness, and most importantly my voice.

Life is a journey, so I'm not saying there isn't more to learn about myself. I'm always evolving. What I'm saying is I'm so content with being Tiffany Renee Booker-James. So many miracles came out of my time in Oakdale. Rich relationships that forever impacted my life. It was like going to the hospital as a precaution after falling and having a CT scan done that revealed pre-existing hemorrhaging in the brain—that very fall actually saved my life. Losing my job and deciding to not work, which led to us losing our home and all that we worked for, actually saved my life.

We remained in Oakdale for ten years and moved at the beginning of this new journey, which includes me writing this book. I've learned we can't always wait until the script is perfect before stepping out on stage and saying, "Here I am!" If you wait, you might not ever step out. Fear of what man thinks will keep you behind the curtain, living with regrets. I'm so glad God pulled the curtain on my life and exposed everything, so I could get rid of what didn't belong in my script.

Now I'm redirecting and realigning my ending. I've heard it said before and I will put it in my own words:

*"The part of you that you are fearful of is the part of you that the enemy does not want the world to see. The fearful part of you is the most powerful part of you."*

## No Limits

THERE IS A MYTH that exists, an untruth that has formed our opinion of who God really is, therefore, shaping our perception of who we are. He's considered a superhero who doesn't really exist, a great legend whose legacy is still spoken of. Some even say He is an illusion of the mind; a great magician of some kind. But I'm here to tell you a great injustice has been done!

We have boxed God into the chambers of our imaginations—imaginations that have been polluted by the reality of this world, therefore becoming the focal point of our stagnations. We have so limited God, like a dream to a sleeper. trapped in between one's subconscious and one's reality only to wake up to see that things aren't what they ought to be. Trapped like a picture within a frame, but just like the clouds can't absorb the rain, He is God and He will no longer be contained.

He is indescribable and uncontainable like a wildfire burning away the layers of debris of whom we've tried to make him out to be, and He's screaming down from the heavens, "Now is the time. Release me."

See, He desires all of Him to be released on the inside of you, but it's going to take you opening yourself up completely to Him in order to get that type of breakthrough. When you're able to see that there are no limits in Him, then and only then can you see that there is none in you and that He's given you everything you need to accomplish what He has set out for you to do.

I need to let you in on a little truth: The only person who can hold you back in this life is you!

See, we can attract anything that our mind can conceive and our heart believes, and let me be very clear—I'm not talking about that nonsense such as Scientology, but faith in the One who made a way for you to survive all hell and still be here today. Faith in the One who says it's never too late, for He is God and He lives outside of the limitations of time and space.

My words are one of a skilled and sharpened writer, cutting away those Pinocchio strings that have been holding you back from walking into your blessing. Yes, it's time to cut away all the limitations.

See, I've come to the conclusion that we can no longer allow ourselves to be labeled by the world's systems, such as Expedia, Experian, or Transunion. Losing our job or even our home will not stop us from one day again having our own. Maturing to the point of understanding that there are some things that do not work out the way we think they should, but I can tell you all things work together for our good.

So let's stop allowing ourselves to be measured by the ruler of society or finding ourselves restricted by the strongholds of religion, trapped by walls of excuses and procrastination, enslaved by the standards of man, imprisoned by past failures, caught up in being a spectator and opinionator of other people's success, and why—when we won't even step out and give our dreams a try?

And let's do away with that old cliché "fake it until you make it." Laughing on the outside while trying to mask the struggle of surviving within, because let it be quiet as kept, all we need to do is remove the mask, humble ourselves, and simply ask for help. Because if we continue to fake it, in the long run we aren't going to make it, and if we continue to complain and point the blame, the problems we're having are sure to remain. So remove the mask and allow your tears to water your desires, drown your doubts, and wash away the boundary lines of yesterday. Let your prayers be the crane that lifts you from your pit while your perseverance pushes back the walls of limits, and let every no you have received become the very force that compels you to create your own yes!

Learn to live in the moment, for the moment's always-present opportunities!

Let's stop trying to make money, competing to make a name for ourselves, and make a difference instead. Don't you know that history shows that great people set out on a journey to speak out for righteousness, break down prejudice, stand for equality, create opportunities, save lives, help the poor, and change the world? They pursued their passion and fulfilled their purpose, and it was their dedication as well as their accomplishments that created their name, and that's why throughout history their legacy remained.

Now I have a question for you: What is your passion calling you to pursue?

When you figure it out, here is what I want you to do: Open your mouth and allow your purpose to speak. For they say every great shout start with a voice, so lift the voice of your gifting and allow the message of your abilities to speak to the world in its own language with unrestricted access, crossing over into the hearts of all of mankind.

Yes, lift your voice up and sing, "I'm a daughter [or son] of the King." From the highest mountain to the deepest blue sea, can't you hear it echoing back at you? "Unlimited possibilities reside on the inside of me, me, and me!"

If you feel that there must be some limitations in your life, then I'm here to tell you I totally agree. So, limit the lies, limit the bad habits, limit unforgiveness, limit the word can't, limit confusion, limit doubt, limit self-pity, limit negativity, limit judgment, limit bitterness, limit ignorance, limit strife, limit pettiness, limit fear, limit compromising, for the time is drawing near, and limit your past so He can extend your future. Remember, you are extraordinary in the eyes of the beholder, and the Beholder is the One and true living

God, the Alpha and the Omega (Beginning and the End), the Creator of the heavens and the earth, the author and finisher of our faith.

He is the God of NO Limits.
The Great I AM.

———————•  •———————

"I AM WHO I AM."

*—God*

CHAPTER TEN

# The Creator of the Land

This chapter is the chapter of all chapters. It's a truth that I declare will open the eyes of your heart. I hope it will answer many unanswered questions.

As I stated before, we all were created on purpose for a purpose because we were created by a God of purpose. Now I don't know what you believe and I'm not trying to even challenge what you believe. I'm sharing my journey of how I discovered the Land of I am—how I learned and embraced my identity.

I want to share how this forty-two-year-old African-American woman from the South Side of Chicago— who felt rejected, who felt ugly as a child, who felt like everything about her was wrong, who felt lost, who struggled with purpose and opposition most of her life, who was molested as a child, who grew to look for love in all the wrong places, who felt used by men, who survived a head-on collision while hoping she would die so that everyone who ever hurt her could feel the wrath of guilt, who never felt comfortable being herself—is now free, smiling, fulfilled, and breathing!

I purposely didn't write about all the things I went through because, again, we all have a story and every story is significant. Every story gives insight to who we are. Yet I believe we often think that the disappointments and the tragedy are the story, and they're not. The true story is self-discovery. It's the purpose for which you and I exist.

I exist because I was a thought in the mind of my heavenly Father. I exist because He created me on purpose for a purpose, and when He created me, my Creator made no mistakes. He did not simply create me to waste me; I was entrusted with something great to give to the world, and so were you.

There are times when the word *Christian* evokes a lot of negative emotions, because it has, in many cases, been attached to a cruel religious system. To many it doesn't stand for the truth of being Christlike, of having the heart of Jesus Christ. In the world's eyes, it no longer carries the same connotation of loving like He loved!

But instead of debating, I choose to speak this powerful truth: I fell in love with Jesus and had a personal encounter with Him at nine years old in the attic, which was my bedroom. I didn't know the theology of God; all I knew was that He existed. At the age of nine, in my room, I wrote these song lyrics:

*God is the one, He is the one for me.*
*He is the one that gets me out of bed.*
*He is the one for me; we can lift Him up higher and higher*
   *and never let Him fall.*
*He can open up our hearts and clean out our souls, and*
   *when I go away*
*I will be up there with Him and I know He, and I know*
   *He, will always be there for me.*

Even at nine years old, I had a deep yet simple understanding of God—He exist.

Now my parents believed in God, but they didn't force us to go to church. We went to a Catholic school when I was younger not because of God and not to become Catholic but because my parents wanted us to have the best education and it just so happen the school that provided that was Catholic. Nevertheless, I was fascinated when the nuns talked about God, but I was too young to fully comprehend all that was being taught to me.

Catholic school taught me the rules of God, but not the heart of Him. Yet I'm still grateful, because it was a foundation for what I already believed in secret: God existed. My father used to say, "Sweetheart, just remember the golden rule and you will be fine in life, and that is 'Do unto others as you would want others to do unto you.'" We had this big, beautiful white Bible on the living room table. As a child, I saw it as a beautiful piece of sacred décor. I don't remember ever opening and reading it with my parents.

So, at a such a young age, how did I know there was God who would always be there for me? How did I know He would open up my heart and clean out my soul? I was not taught that, but at age nine, or maybe even earlier than that, I believed it with every ounce of my being. Some have asked me how this is all possible. I tell them, for me, Christianity is not about a certain way of thinking and behaving; it has and will always be about a personal relationship with God, who loves you. I never wrote the song down, but I can still remember every word and the melody to it.

While I was attending the Catholic school, I had a friend who was attending only for the education; as a matter of fact, neither she nor her family believed in God. They believed in the big bang theory. Since then, I have heard about many who believe the same thing, and the questions that I respectfully ask are "Do you really believe there was a cosmic explosion and we were created with the most beautiful features and that each of the features serve a purpose? Do you really believe that an explosion could give us joy, sadness, love, peace, and kindness?"

Many can't answer the questions, and even when people do have an answer, it always leads to another question.

Recently, I was in Calistoga, California, with my friends having a miniature vacation, and decided to try a mud bath for the first time. (I will never do again! Mud got lost in places that I didn't even know it could reach.) Afterward, I had a thirty-minute massage and the masseuse asked me a series of questions. One was, "Are there any areas that you have had problems with?" I said, "Not any longer," which prompted another question: "What happened?"

I told her how my back was miraculously healed by God through prayer. She said, "Wow, energy always heals," or something like that. Again, I respect everyone's spiritual journey, so I didn't try to challenge what she believed or convince her otherwise. As we finished up and were standing outside the door in the hallway waiting on my friend to finish with her massage, the masseuse shared with me that in Calistoga many people believe in the energy god. She went on to say that there was really no difference in what she believed and what I believed.

I responded with one simple question: "Can energy love you back?" She had no answer. I thanked her for an amazing massage, tipped her, and gave her a huge smile, and we said our goodbyes.

She is an amazing woman who I hope has really pondered that question. I was so appreciative that she allowed me to share, because most times it's okay for everyone to boldly share what they believe but if you say the name of Jesus, it's offensive to people. I don't really understand why.

I don't know how else to explain that who I am is a direct result of the One who created me. I don't have the answers to all the theological questions, although I can answer some, but I choose not to argue or debate my faith. I choose to share and impart where my hope comes from. You don't have to agree with it or accept it, but I do ask that people respect what I believe and of course I will do the same for them.

In saying that, I don't believe energy can give you purpose or has the ability to love you or touch the inner part of your being in a way that satisfies your soul. I have tried positive thinking and it worked for a season, but when I was hurting, there wasn't enough positive thinking in the world that could heal the broken pieces of my life. I've read so many books that were excellent and gave me tools that I still use today, but these books didn't transform me. They simply helped me make better decisions with the knowledge I gained.

Nothing, and I mean *nothing*, has spoken to my heart like my heavenly Father. Nothing has had the power to transform me but the power of His love. The peace that I have comes from Him, the joy that I have—even when things are not going right—comes from only Him. At times, people have asked me how I can still be happy while in a bad situation. I say, "I can't be. Happiness is temporary, and it's based on what you have and don't have. It is based on who you have in your life and who you don't have. It is based on what's working or not working in your life."

When situations arise that aren't in my favor, I may not be happy, but I can still be joyful. Joy comes from my Creator. It flows from my being because I know He is always with me, and that I am always loved no matter what. My Creator makes me feel whole and complete. I don't look to anyone or anything else to fulfill me. I'm not saying I don't desire those things; I do. But those things no longer determine my value. I am free because God gave His son Jesus so I can be free and live in the Land of I am all the days of my life.

I finally understand and embrace my purpose. I was created to be a voice crying out in the wilderness. I have the power to speak to the dry places in the hearts of people who are open. I get to give hope to those in hopeless situations. I get to water the seeds of greatness on the inside of them—to see the golden nuggets underneath the hardened soil of their hearts. Yes, I get to look into their eyes and really see them, to help them pull back the curtain and take a bow because

God used their lives to tell a powerful story of His love and redemption. I was created to be a voice of healing, to encourage you into your destiny by first helping you discover your true identity.

Our voices have an authority—yes, a unique sound that speaks its purpose into the world. I get to be an ambassador of God's love. I will never apologize for being me again.

On the day I looked in the mirror beyond what was staring back at me, a smile came over my face. I was able to fully embrace the woman who stood before me. I was breathing on my own for the first time. Yes, in that moment I didn't need anything outside myself to feel complete.

I will never apologize for speaking love into a hateful world, and I will never apologize for fighting for the underdog. I will never apologize for choosing to see the best in everyone instead of labeling them because of their actions. I will never apologize for being a voice to the voiceless, I will never apologize for my belief in God, I will never apologize for not agreeing with the majority but with truth, and I will never apologize for forgiving people when others say I am stupid for doing so. The list can go on and on.

For all of you reading this book, I pray that you feel the touch of Jesus so that you can comprehend with your spirit and not with your head how much He loves us. See, the One who created me lives inside of me. He has been relentless for me since my conception. I was a thought in His heart and so were you, a thought that birthed into a promise. Yes, Jesus thought about you and is still mindful of you. He dreams about and for you. He delights in you and sings over you. He fights over you and for you, and He declares over you and longs to speak to you and through you. There is not a moment that you're not in His sight.

I know many will ask, "If there's a God, why did He allow me to go through the things I've gone through?" That's such a broad question that I will never be able to truly answer. There are some things that I don't know or understand myself, but I choose to trust God's plan and His character. Moreover, during those hard and unexplainable times in life, I rather go through them with God, who is my hope, than without Him. I also strongly believe that if I, in my limited human knowledge, can totally figure the all-powerful God out, then He ceases to be God.

For me, it's a little simpler now that I'm a mother. First, my parents did some things that I thought were unfair, mean, and even weird, but now looking back through my parent lenses, I understand that those decisions were for my good. I now make some decisions that cause my kids to question, complain, get mad, and even question my love for them, but I know they're for their good. I realize that no matter what I say, until they mature or until that situation works itself out, they'll continue to believe a lie that I don't love them, cherish them, and sacrifice for them. For a season they might think and live their life feeling less loved, which again is a lie straight from the pit of hell, because my kids are my world. My girls must learn to trust me even when they don't fully understand me. They must believe in me during the times when they think my actions are against them instead of for them.

Second, when I was younger, I made choices that were not for my best, despite my parents many attempts to guide me with wisdom. Some of those choices brought about consequences beyond their control. I had to learn to be accountable for my decisions and not to blame them, God, the world, or anyone else. There were times I asked for things, or for permission to do things I desired to do, but my parents knew I wasn't mature enough to handle those things. It wasn't about them punishing or being mean to me; as a matter of fact, they were protecting me.

So many times, we say, "I prayed for [this or that]." I don't know about you, but I can certainly tell you many of the things I prayed for, I was *not* ready for. You want to know how I know? I know because sometimes I forced my own way and had to deal with the consequences of my not-so-good choice. Those consequences spoke loud and clear that I was not ready for it.

Last, there is an enemy in this world and that enemy is the devil. He comes to kill, steal, and destroy. With all the hate, cruelty, sadness, sickness, anger, deceit, perversion, wickedness, and so much more around us, you can't deny that the devil is real.

We can't blame everything on God. Yes, we can ask why He allows some things to happen. But then if He controlled everything, if He didn't give us free will, many would say that makes God a mean dictator. Then we would still have a problem with God.

In the movie *God's Not Dead*, there is an intense debate between a professor who believes in evolution and a college student who believes in God. The young man is questioning the professor when the debate comes to a halt and the professor states that God never did anything for him and that he's mad at God. The young man asks how he can be mad at someone he doesn't believe exists. It takes faith to believe that there isn't a God and that our existence is of some other occurrence.

I believe that one day Jesus who lives in me will bring me face-to-face with the One who created me—the GREAT I AM. He is where I live! I live, move, and have my being in Him. I never try to force anyone to believe what I believe, but I always give an invitation to know the Great I AM personally. I want everyone, including you, to experience the love, peace, wholeness, and freedom that I have come to live in. The reality is that He has given us all a choice, and I know He will be relentless for you just like he was for me. I pray that you choose Him, but even if you don't, that will never stop Him from loving you.

It grieves me when my kids pull away from me, and I know it grieves His heart when we pull away from Him. However, I could never stop loving my kids, no matter what they do, and He will never stop loving us.

Love is the universal thing that every human being longs for. Love is not weak, it bows down to no one but surrenders itself to everyone by its own authority. It is the one thing that the land must have, the one thing that the land can't survive without, and the one thing that allows the land to flourish. Yes, you can tend your garden, pulling all the weeds of comparison, unforgiveness, pain, hate, bitterness, sadness, and whatever else that hinders you from growing, but the land will not be able to sustain itself without love.

Living in the Land of I am is ultimately living in Him being your true authentic self, living in His Love for He is Love. Living, moving, and having your creative being in Him. Everyone has an innate desire to love and be loved, and when you don't have love, your identity is blurred. They go hand in hand like peanut butter and jelly, like cake and frosting, like mashed potatoes and gravy, and like a horse and carriage. You are eternally loved and accepted, created in the image and likeness of God. Like water is to the soil, so is love to the soul. You can't live without it. Love will never be silent. It will always raise its voice to truth, and when everything else is gone, love will be the last thing standing! It will outlive everything including the land itself, but while you are here, remain rooted and grounded in love.

God is love and it is the best soil (foundation) that makes everything possible in the Land of I am.

I pray that each of you chooses to live in the Land of I am and to ask the GREAT I AM to establish you in that land (that truth) that being you is enough. You were created on purpose for a purpose! You can find your destiny once you know your identity. I have prayed for every person who is reading this book. There is more to you than meets the eye, and I am cheering for you.

THIS LAST INSPIRATIONAL PIECE is by far one of the most profound pieces God has written upon my heart. I know that I AM is the name that God has given Himself, for He is truly the Great I AM. With that in mind, I am not referring to myself as I AM, but simply stating that I am is a powerful statement of being whomever God created us to be with no limits or labels attached. I am His creation birthed from the womb of His Spirit and so are you. We are created in the image and likeness of God with everything within us to fulfill the purpose for which we were created. So, as you read this piece, read it as a statement and not the name of God. This is my "I am" statement.

It's time for you to find, acknowledge, and embrace your own "I am" statement.

# I am

I AM THE LIVING word birthed from the womb of my Creator's Spirit ... unexpected yet I was predestined ... never a mistake! I was divinely purposed. I am.

I am not a fictional character in a book, or an actress playing a role in a movie scene. Neither am I a fleeting thought that races across your mind. I exist!

I am not a game piece on a on a chess board. No one determines my next move. I can't be minimized by words, wished away with three wishes, and once again, you can't ignore my existence, for my vibration has been released into the atmosphere.

Yes, I live in the unseen places of your mind, desired in the innermost places of your being.

It is where truth prevails, therefore I am.

I am a provoking, vulnerable teardrop from heaven. Feel the refreshing touch of my presence. I am as strong as the horns of a bull charging through. Feel the strength of spirit lifting you. I am as numerous as the sand on the banks of the ocean shore. I can't be traced, contained, or ignored. I am.

I am the highest peak of any mountain. Hear the echo of my inspiration. For I declare the handiwork of my Father's creation.

I am the footsteps of wisdom, hear me coming—the lion of Judah, hear me roaring. I am the thunderous power of His Praise ... who can stand against me!

I am the stirring in your belly, the overflow of your river, the repellent to your fears, the moon in your midnight hour. Let me shine. I am.

I am the calm, slow drip of rain on a hot summer day.

I am the force of encouragement ripping through the disappoint of your soul.

I am the segue to your dreams, your eyes in the darkness when you can't see.

In the most violent storm, I am your serenity. I am.

I am the clarity to your confusion, the conflict in your compromise, the heartbeat to your compassion, the freedom in your song, the assassin to your doubts, your champion to your faith.

I was created for you. I am.

I am often misunderstood, always underestimated, yet I am the exclamation mark behind my own validation.

I am the start point, the runner, and the finish line of my destiny. I am a thoroughbred.

Study my stance, watch me run. I was born to win.

I am the capital letter of His promise and the period behind His purpose. Yes, I live outside and within my Creator's beginning and end. I'm the comma in the middle of your spirit—pause, breathe, listen, and receive. For I am the key to unlock destinies. And I am not confined to time, for I live in eternity. Therefore, I am a never-ending story. He lived, I died; He died, I lived. Therefore I am.

I am the reality of my Creator, the impression of His spirit, the leap of His joy. I am His voice crying out in the wilderness. I am His answer to your concern, His fertilizer to a dying world. I am the responsibility and radiance of His love.

I am the shadow of His wings; you can take refuge in me. I am His message in a bottle, just like Him I have broken for you. I am the oxygen to the soul. I am His warrior that ends the war. I am.

I am the bend of His will, His secret in the secret place. His mystery lives within me; that's why I don't accept meager possibilities. For everything I need to reign in this life is in me. Search, seek, knock, and you shall find that you were the prize desired in the Creator's eyes.

He lived, you died; He died, you live. Therefore, you too are I am.

HE IS THE GREAT I AM
I am THE GREAT I AM'S
I AM THAT I AM.

———————————• •———————————

# ENDNOTES

[1] Steve Harvey, Twitter post, September 25, 2015, 5:24 p.m., accessed October 16, 2018, https://twitter.com/iamsteveharvey/status/383024206679535616?lang=en.

[2] *Encarta World English Dictionary* (New York: St. Martin's Press, 2004), *s.v.* "different."

[3] "Steve Jobs > Quotes," *Goodreads*, accessed August 20, 2018, http://www.goodreads.com/quotes/463176-you-can-t-connect-the-dots-looking-forward-you-can-only.

[4] Marianne Williamson, *A Return to Love: Reflections on the Principals of A Course in Miracles* (New York: HarperCollins, 1992), 190–191.

[5] *Dictionary.com, s.v.* "potential," accessed August 22, 2018, http://www.dictionary.com/browse/potential?s=t.

[6] "Quotes > Sidney Poitier," *AZ Quotes*, accessed August 22, 2018, https://www.azquotes.com/quote/373517.

[7] *Merriam-Webster Online Dictionary, s.v.* "greatness," accessed August 22, 2018, https://www.merriam-webster.com/thesaurus/greatness.

[8] Asad Meah, "23 Inspirational Greatness Quotes," *Awaken the Greatness Within*, accessed October 16, 2018, https://awaken thegreatnesswithin.com/23-inspirational-greatness-quotes/.

[9] "Aurora Greenaway Quotes, Quotations & Sayings," *SearchQuotes*, accessed December 3, 2018, http://www.search quotes.com/search/Aurora_Greenway/.

[10] Antonia Blumberg, "Rev. Martin Luther King Jr.: 'A Riot Is The Language Of The Unheard,'" *Huffington Post*, April 29, 2015, Accessed August 28, 2018, https://www.huffingtonpost.com/2015/04/28/martin-luther-king-riot_n_7160380.html.

[11] *Oxford Living Dictionaries, s.v.* "perception," accessed October 16, 2018, https://en.oxforddictionaries.com/definition/perception.

[12] "(1982) Audre Lorde, 'Learning from the 60s,'" Blackpast.org, accessed October 16, 2018, https://blackpast.org/1982-audr e-lorde-learning-60s.

62173194R00095

Made in the USA
Columbia, SC
30 June 2019